THE BOSTON
TEA PARTY

*COLONISTS PROTEST
THE BRITISH GOVERNMENT*

MILESTONES
IN AMERICAN HISTORY

MILESTONES
IN
AMERICAN HISTORY

THE BOSTON TEA PARTY

*COLONISTS PROTEST
THE BRITISH GOVERNMENT*

SAMUEL WILLARD CROMPTON

CHELSEA HOUSE
An Infobase Learning Company

The Boston Tea Party

Copyright © 2011 by Infobase Learning

Chelsea House
An imprint of Infobase Learning
132 West 31st Street
New York, NY 10001

Library of Congress Cataloging-in-Publication Data

Crompton, Samuel Willard.
Boston Tea Party : colonists protest the British government / by Samuel Willard Crompton.
  p. cm. — (Milestones in American history)
Includes bibliographical references and index.
ISBN 978-1-60413-764-4 (hardcover)
1. Boston Tea Party, 1773—Juvenile literature. I. Title. II. Series.

E215.7.C76 2011
973.3'115—dc22   2011004461

Chelsea House books are available at special discounts when purchased in bulk quantities for businesses, associations, institutions, or sales promotions. Please call our Special Sales Department in New York at (212) 967-8800 or (800) 322-8755.

You can find Chelsea House on the World Wide Web at http://www.infobaselearning.com

Text design by Erik Lindstrom
Cover design by Alicia Post
Composition by Keith Trego
Cover printed by Yurchak Printing, Landisville, Pa.
Book printed and bound by Yurchak Printing, Landisville, Pa.
Date printed: August 2011
Printed in the United States of America

10 9 8 7 6 5 4 3 2 1

This book is printed on acid-free paper.

All links and Web addresses were checked and verified to be correct at the time of publication. Because of the dynamic nature of the Web, some addresses and links may have changed since publication and may no longer be valid.

CONTENTS

Sons of Liberty, Sons of Violence

A British lady, who had just moved to Boston, wrote to her London correspondent on June 30, 1768. The letter was postmarked from Castle William in Boston Harbor:

> Dear Madam,
>
> I presume it will be agreeable to you to hear that my brother's family had a good voyage of 5 weeks & arrived all well at Boston the 5th instant [the fifth of June]. You will be surprised to hear how we were obliged to fly from the place in six days after & take refuge on board the *Romney*, man of war lying in Boston Harbor.[1]

Miss Ann Hulton, whose brother was Henry Hulton, the new collector of customs in Boston, had arrived at a time when that town and the surrounding countryside were in an uproar over taxes, customs duties, and tea.

Mrs. Burch, at whose house I was, had frequently been alarmed with the Sons of Liberty surrounding her house with [the] most hideous howlings as the Indians, when they attack an enemy, to many insults & outrages she had been exposed since her arrival, & threatened with greater violences. She had removed her most valuable effects & held herself in readiness to depart at an hours notice.[2]

This was a constant for British officials and American loyalists in Boston. The Boston crowd, or mob, could be whipped up at the notice of an hour or two, and it was the loyal supporters of King George III and the British parliament that suffered the brunt of their aggressions.

The occasion soon happened, when my sister & I accompanied her at 10 o'clock at night to a neighbors' house, not apprehending much danger, but we soon found that the mobs here are very different from those in Old England where a few lights put into the windows will pacify, or the interposition of a magistrate restrain them, but here they *act from principle & under countenance* [emphasis added], no person daring or willing to suppress their outrages.[3]

Even from the distance of two and a half centuries, we can hear the sneer in the words "act from principle & under countenance." To Ann Hulton, and other British persons, the Sons of Liberty (whom she called the "Sons of Violence"[4]) did not have any principles at all. She did notice, however, that they acted "under countenance," meaning that the Boston public officials did nothing to stop them.

Ann Hulton had arrived at a time of crisis.

THE TOWNSHEND ACTS

Just a year earlier, Boston and most of the American colonies had lain rather quiet under British government. The furor over

In 1765, American colonists in Boston rioted in protest against the Stamp Act, a tax instituted by King George and the British parliament. The Stamp Act was repealed, but the British government continued to implement new taxes on the colonies.

the much-hated Stamp Act had subsided when that act was repealed by the British parliament. But in 1767, Parliament and King George had laid a set of taxes (whether they were taxes or customs duties was a subject of debate) on the colonies. Paper, painter's colors, glass, lead, and tea had all received new taxes, some of which were fairly light and some of which were rather heavy.

Although virtually all American seaport towns demonstrated resistance to the Townshend Revenue Acts, Boston, as was so often the case, was the loudest. The town was divided between a prosperous upper class, which delighted in the drinking of tea, and a rather marginal middle class, which was turning to ale, beer, and other beverages. Of course, there was a third, truly desperate, section of Boston's population, the people that lived practically from hand to mouth, but few of them left records of their political leanings because they were too occupied in the struggle to survive.

In 1768, Boston was a town of 16,000 persons, many of whom claimed descent from the first Puritan settlers of 1630. It was a rather homogeneous place, with most of its inhabitants carrying Anglo-Saxon names like Carpenter, Russell, Fairweather, and Adams. Had King George and the British parliament given up their plans to tax the American colonies, they would have found few places of stronger loyalty than Boston and the surrounding towns. But because Boston was a commercial place, one where the people lived or died according to the quality of the merchant trade, Bostonians could not bear to see any new taxes from Old England.

THE GOVERNOR AND THE LADY

Miss Ann Hulton wrote to her London correspondent again on July 12, 1768. She and her brother's family were still at Castle William in Boston Harbor (it is Castle Island today). They had to remain in the safety of Castle William because the Boston mob was in a great uproar over the recent seizure of a merchant ship belonging to John Hancock, the Boston merchant who would later sign the Declaration of Independence.

> This is our situation, & you are not to imagine us though in a state of banishment, secluded from society or the rest of the world, it is rather like one of the public water drinking places in England. We have a great many visitors come every day from Boston incognito, & are seldom less than twenty at dinner. We live luxuriously though I don't find provisions so cheap as I expected, but I believe We Government people pay dearer.[5]

This was, and is, a complaint frequently expressed by those in the diplomatic service of all nations: The customary rates for bread, meat, and lodgings increase when the locals know that one has a deep pocket. Perhaps the most interesting part of the July 12 letter came at the very end: "Governor Bernard has just now drunk tea here with us. His Excellency says [that] two more such years as in the past & the British Empire is at an end."[6]

Perhaps it is only a coincidence that Miss Hulton, Governor Francis Bernard, and their companions drank *tea* that day, but it shows a marked difference from the Americans ashore, in Boston proper, for tea was becoming off limits to patriotic Americans. King George and Parliament had placed a tax of three pennies per pound of tea, and many Americans were in the process of giving up the Chinese tea leaves, of which they had been so fond.

One cannot say for certain, but one suspects that if Samuel Adams and the Sons of Liberty gathered that same day, or week, that they would have lifted cups and bumpers of *ale* rather than tea, and that the difference in beverages was becoming a sign of the difference between patriot and Loyalist. As to Governor Bernard's statement, 1768 would not mark the end of the British Empire in America, but it did mark a departure in British-American relations, for just a few months later came the first regiments of red-coated British soldiers.

Boston was about to become an occupied town.

King George and His Parliament

George II, king of England, Scotland, Ireland, and a fair part of North America, died on October 25, 1760. His reign had lasted almost 33 years.

George, the Prince of Wales, became King George III immediately on the death of his grandfather (his father had died several years earlier). The official coronation was not until the spring of 1761, but George III quickly took the reins of government.

The situation, as he saw it, was very good indeed. Recent British triumphs over its French foe had made England mistress of the seas, and close to master of the land.

THE MIRACLE YEAR(S)

In English history, 1759 is known as the Year of Miracles, the one in which British sailors chased French sailors from the ocean, and when British soldiers won key battles that ensured the expansion of the British Empire. To be fully accurate, however, one would need to characterize *both* 1757 and 1759 as miracle years, for in the former Britain won control of much of India and in the latter she gained sway over all of Canada.

On June 23, 1757, Major General Robert Clive (later known as Clive of India) won the Battle of Plassey in far-off Bengal. He was allied with several Indian leaders who fought against the French and their Indian allies. Clive's victory at Plassey ensured that England would play a leading role in the affairs of India for decades to come. The coast of India became filled with warehouses of the British East India Company, which imported tea from China, then sent it on to England.

On September 13, 1759, Major General James Wolfe won the Battle of the Plains of Abraham, just outside Quebec City. Thirty-one-year-old Wolfe was wounded three times during the short battle, and he collapsed toward its end, asking his men who had won the day. When they told him the French were in full retreat, Wolfe said something to the effect that now he could die in peace (Benjamin West later executed a famous painting of the scene).

Quebec City surrendered four days later, and the French flag was hauled down, to be replaced by the British Union Jack. Robert Clive and James Wolfe became among the best known of all British heroes; some say that their fame was not eclipsed until the time of Lord Kitchener of Khartoum (more than a century later). Though they did not know each other, and though their conquests were continents apart, Robert Clive and James Wolfe paved the way for what historians often call the "First British Empire" to distinguish it from the one later established during the time of Queen Victoria.

Though it was not immediately apparent, the British victories at Plassey and the Plains of Abraham both played a role in bringing about the Boston Tea Party, and, later, the American Revolution. The East India Company—whose fortunes were made possible by Clive's victory—would ship tea to American colonies that felt less fear of the French (or anyone else) since the conquest of Canada, which was made possible by Wolfe's victory.

THE PEACE OF PARIS

George III received his formal coronation in 1761, and by 1763, when the Peace of Paris was signed, British predominance in the wider world was assured. Under the terms of the treaty, England received all of Canada from the French, all of Florida from the Spanish, and territorial rights to a large section of India and Bengal. Just as important, the British were now unrivaled at sea; their merchant marine could exploit the colonies and territories, bringing all sorts of merchandise from different parts of the globe.

King George was fully aware of the grandeur of England and her brilliant status in the world, but he also knew that the British national debt had swelled to an alarming number: 167 million pounds sterling. There is no way to make an exact comparison between this figure and the United States national debt of our time; suffice to say that paying the interest on the national debt consumed about *half* of the entire British revenue on a yearly basis. As he looked at the situation, King George decided—with the help of his ministers—that the American colonies should pay a portion, however small, of the national debt because the French and Indian War (as the Seven Years' War was called in America) had been fought for their benefit.

Americans disagreed.

WRITS OF ASSISTANCE AND THE SUGAR ACT

Even before the Seven Years' War ended, King George's ministers enacted the so-called writs of assistance that allowed customs officials to enter the homes of Americans to make sure they were not smuggling goods. The American colonists had

King George III became monarch during a time of success and prosperity for Britain. This success, however, caused the British Empire to fall into debt and the new king believed the American colonists should help pay a portion of it.

proved remarkably astute at avoiding the payment of customs duties, and King George wanted to make sure that his revenue officers were able to collect what was owed to the Crown.

When the law of the writs of assistance became public, Americans registered mild protests, but in a port town—one that prided itself on its commercial success—there was a strong response. James Otis, a native of Cape Cod and a resident of Boston, argued against the writs of assistance in the

JAMES OTIS

No one knows which American first shouted "no representation without taxation," but James Otis (1725–1783) comes close.

"The natural liberty of man is to be free from any superior power on earth, and not to be under the will or legislative authority of man, but only to have the law of nature as his rule. . . . The Colonists being men, have a right to be considered as equally entitled to all the rights of nature with the Europeans, and they are not to be restrained in the exercise of any of these rights, but for the evident good of the community."*

King George and the British parliament would not have agreed, but James Otis was writing on behalf of his fellow American colonists. Otis did not dislike the British system of government—far from it; but he believed that Americans were being denied the full exercise of their rights as British subjects.

"There is no foundation for the distinction some make in England, between an internal and an external tax on the colonies. By the first is meant a tax on trade, by the latter a tax on land, and the things on it. A tax on trade is either a tax of every man in the province, or 'tis not. If 'tis not a tax on the whole, 'tis unequal and unjust, that a heavy burden should be laid on the trade of the colonies, to maintain an army of soldiers, custom-house officers, and fleets of guard-ships." **

Massachusetts superior court. Though he lost the case, Otis used his arguments that day as the basis for his famous pamphlet, *The Rights of the British Colonies Asserted and Proved.*

At about the time that James Otis's pamphlet was printed, Americans learned that King George's government had

Otis was going a bit far; no one had suggested that the writs of assistance, or any other law would be used to fund an army in the colonies. But for his readers, especially those in Boston, his arguments rang true.

"This constitution [the British one] is the most free one, and by far the best, now existing on earth: that by this constitution, every man in the dominions is a free man: that no part of His Majesty's dominions can be taxed without their consent: that every part has a right to be represented in the supreme or some subordinate legislature."***

Like many other Americans, James Otis believed in the British constitution, which had evolved over hundreds of years, since the time of the Magna Carta. What he did not believe in was the right of the king and Parliament to tax the colonies, since the colonies were not represented in Parliament. Otis may not have used the exact words "taxation without representation," but he came close enough to be called one of the founders of the idea, and the ideal, of American liberty.

---

*Morison, S.E., editor. *Sources and Documents Illustrating the American Revolution, 1764–1788*. Oxford, England: The Clarendon Press, 1923, p. 5.
**Ibid., p. 6.
***Ibid., pp. 8–9.

amended the Sugar, or Molasses, Act of 1733. The new legislation actually reduced the amount of customs duty to be paid, but it also made it easier for royal officials to enforce the collection. Americans did not react strongly to the amendment of the Sugar Act, which had been in operation for many years, but they were first distressed, and then furious, when they learned of the Stamp Act in 1765.

STAMPS AND COLLECTORS

Americans had long escaped direct taxation: They had paid customs duties (or avoided them by smuggling) but had never been taxed by Parliament in their properties. This changed with the Stamp Act, which Parliament approved in March 1765.

Contracts, deeds, wills, newspapers, and even something so innocent as a pack of playing cards—any and all printed material would have to bear the king's stamp, which could only be obtained from his revenue officers. There was already a stamp act in England, Scotland, and Ireland, but the legislation of 1765 extended it to the American colonies.

One can argue that townspeople—such as the Bostonians or New Yorkers—were harmed more than their country fellows, because of the amount of printed material in the coastal towns, but what struck everyone was the unanimity of the opposition. Americans, from New Hampshire to South Carolina, condemned the Stamp Act as the first direct tax and as a symbol of British tyranny (Georgia, the last of the colonies to be founded, did not see any protests of the Stamp Act). King George, who had been quite popular when he succeeded to the throne, suddenly became known as a royal tyrant.

Boston, New York, Newport, Rhode Island, Philadelphia, and Charles Town, South Carolina, led the way in resisting the Stamp Act. In Boston, an organization called the Sons of Liberty sprang into being within weeks of people learning of the Stamp Act. In Manhattan, the equivalent organization was called the Liberty Boys. Philadelphia was a bit more quiet, but

Charles Town had its own organization of patriots, and it was among the first towns to designate a certain tree as the "Liberty Tree" or "Liberty Pole;" the idea spread to other towns throughout the colonies.

Boston led the way. In August 1765, a group of the Sons of Liberty brought the local Stamp Act collector to the Liberty Tree, bound and gagged him, threatened his life, and eventually persuaded him to resign his office. Ten days later, another Sons of Liberty group attacked the mansion of the unpopular lieutenant governor, practically destroying it. Some of the organization's leaders recognized this wanton act of violence as a mistake because it undermined the claim of the colonists that they were standing for their rights as law-abiding citizens. Though there would be plenty of threats of violence in the days and weeks ahead, no more homes were attacked.

REPEAL

During the winter of 1765–1766, King George and the leaders of Parliament got an earful of complaints, both from the American colonies and the leading merchants of London. It was obvious that the Americans hated the Stamp Act; less obvious was that the British merchants agreed because it was already reducing trade with America (a number of Americans were boycotting British goods). On March 4, 1766, Parliament voted to rescind (repeal) the Stamp Act, and King George gave the royal assent.

When news of the repeal reached the colonies, Americans gave way to expressions of joy. So popular did George III suddenly become that the town of New York voted to fund the creation of a statue of the king, which stood near what is now Broadway (it was pulled down during the Revolution). It was around this time that a myth, or fallacy, developed, the idea that King George was on the side of his colonists while his ministers and the leaders of Parliament were not. As mistaken as this belief was, it lasted for a number of years.

The first direct British tax imposed upon American colonists came in the form of the Stamp Act. All printed materials in the colonies had to be printed on expensive paper featuring the royal stamp (*above left and center*), and was only available for purchase from revenue officers. The stamp on the right is a newspaper satire of the enforced stamps.

Americans chose to overlook another piece of legislation, voted and passed on the same day that the Stamp Act was rescinded. Parliament voted in favor of the Declaratory Act, which asserted the right of the king and Parliament to legislate for the colonies in all cases whatsoever. This obviously included taxation.

The Sons of Liberty, the Liberty Boys, and other organizations did not disband, but there seemed less need for them in the year that followed. King George remained popular in the colonies, and no one took much notice of British affairs until the summer of 1767, when it was learned that another set of customs duties were about to be imposed on the colonies.

TOWNSHEND ACTS

Charles Townshend, the chancellor of the Exchequer of Great Britain, believed that the Americans would not resist customs duties, as opposed to direct taxes. There was some truth in his belief, in that Americans were used to the idea of customs duties. But when the Townshend Revenue Acts were announced, many Americans denounced them as tyrannical on a par with the Stamp Act. Bostonians received their first news of the Townshend Acts in October 1767:

> For every 112 pounds of crown, plate, flint, and white
>   glass, 4 shillings, 8 pence
> For every 112 pounds of green glass, 1 shilling 2 pence
> For every 112 pounds of red lead, 2 shillings
> For every 112 pounds of painter's colors, 2 shillings,
> For every pound of tea, 3 pence.[1]

Of all the Townshend Acts, the one on tea was the smallest, just three pence, but it was the one that caused the most commotion. Just two months later, Bostonians read in their local paper of a new way to obtain tea:

> The use of Hyperion or Labradore Tea, is every day coming into more general vogue among people of all ranks. The virtues of this plant or shrub from which this delicate tea is gathered, were first discovered by the Aborigines, and from them the Canadians learned them. It soon became into such repute that quantities were sent to France; where I have heard say, it was soon in such demand, as alarmed the French East India Company, and procured an ordinance prohibiting the importation of any more on the pain of death.[2]

The newspaper essay doubtless exaggerated to some extent, but the American colonists were eager to find something, anything that would avoid the three-pence tax per pound of imported tea. After some time they found that the new Labradore tea lacked the strong caffeine punch of the leaves imported from China, but Americans continued to experiment with different types of beverages.

BOSTON RESISTS

In the spring of 1768, Boston received a new customs commissioner (Henry Hulton) and a beefed-up presence was noticed among the few soldiers in town. When Hulton and other customs men seized the *Liberty*, a sloop belonging to John Hancock, a prominent merchant and a member of the Sons of Liberty, Boston went into an uproar, bringing the commotion that Ann Hulton noticed when she first came to America.

Governor Francis Bernard was already weary of the Americans and their constant talk of liberty, freedom, and privileges. As a last effort to maintain the king's power in Boston, Governor Bernard asked for two regiments of British troops, which arrived on the first of October 1768.

The Boston Massacre

Paul Revere (1735–1818) was a silversmith, a message runner, and an engraver, who parlayed his many skills into earning a living for his large family. He lived in the Old North End of Boston, where his house is now a tourist attraction.

On October 1, 1768, Paul Revere saw two regiments of British soldiers come ashore. He quickly made an engraving of the event, and copies were sent throughout the colonies. One might say it was the first illustration to become almost universal with everyday Americans. Revere entitled the engraving "A View of Part of the Town of Boston in New England and British Ships of War Landing their Troops." He dedicated the engraving to "the Earl of Hillsborough, His Majesty's secretary of state for America. This view of the only well planned expedition formed *for supporting the dignity of Britain & chastising the insolence of America* [emphasis added] is humbly inscribed."[1]

Just as the reader of today can hear the sneer behind Ann Hulton's use of "act from principle & under countenance," so can one hear the anger and the irony in Paul Revere's phrase "for supporting the dignity of Britain & chastising the insolence of America."

OCCUPATION

The British soldiers, totaling about a thousand, marched to Boston Common to pitch their tents because there were no barracks in town. Some of the troops went to Castle William for the winter, but others were quartered on the populace. To be quartered meant that the soldiers lived in the houses of selected Boston families who had to provide bed and breakfast for the men. Needless to say, this move did not endear the soldiers to Bostonians.

NONIMPORTATION

At the same time that Britain sent soldiers to Boston, many Americans began another boycott of British goods. The Townshend Acts were placed only on paper, paint, glass, lead, and tea, but some Americans went further, refusing to purchase anything made in Old England until the acts were removed. The historian T.H. Breen expresses it thus:

> No one knows when precisely American public opinion first realized that imported goods provided powerful political leverage within the empire. Such discoveries usually result from a slow, cumulative conviction that the taken-for-granted of everyday life has possibilities that no one only a few years earlier quite perceived. But insomuch as there was a moment when inchoate thoughts about consumer dependence crystallized into firm belief, it occurred in mid-February 1766.[2]

That was at the height of the Stamp Act controversy, a time when many Americans were boycotting, or about to boycott,

British goods. Breen argues that between 1766 and 1769, thousands, perhaps hundreds of thousands, of Americans realized the leverage they had, because British manufacturers needed markets for their goods. The Stamp Act was dead and gone by 1768, but Americans now railed against the Townshend Acts, and in the summer of 1769 the nonimportation movement scored some startling successes. Boston's role in such a movement was almost taken for granted, but that Virginians, under the leadership of George Washington, adopted their own form of nonimportation was startling. British merchants reported an alarming drop in orders from the colonies, whether for paper, paint, glass, lead, tea, or anything else.

TENSIONS BUILD

The winter of 1769–1770 was not especially harsh (Americans had noted a moderation of their climate over the previous three decades), but the presence of a thousand British soldiers led to tensions in Boston. Quite a few of the soldiers decided to "moonlight," to earn extra money by performing civilian tasks, and in so doing they took work away from regular Bostonians, who had already suffered from an economic recession over the past few years.

Much of our knowledge of Boston at that time comes from the essays and poems of well-to-do persons, but there is a rather rare source that shows Boston, and its irritation with the British, from a working-class perspective. George Robert Twelve Hewes (his full name) was a shoemaker who had struggled with poverty for some years. He and his wife had a number of children, and the shoemaking trade was not enough to support them. Later in life—when interviewed by a New York journalist—Hewes related his memory of the winter of 1769–1770 and the Boston Massacre. "On my enquiring of Hewes what knowledge he had of that event, he replied, that he knew nothing from history, as he had never read anything relating to it from any publication whatever, and can therefore

Tensions between British soldiers and the local colonists reached a breaking point on the night of the Boston Massacre in 1770. As the civilians harassed the British regiment, several confused soldiers fired their weapons and killed five Bostonians.

only give the information that I derived from the event of the day upon which the catastrophe happened."[3]

Hewes happened to see a British officer enter a barbershop, where his hair was cut by the apprentice boy rather than the regular shop owner. Apparently, the officer left without paying his bill, and the boy pursued him to the house where he lived, only to be turned away by the sentry at the door. Very likely this did not cause the riot that happened later in the day, but it may have added fuel to the fire that already existed. We know from other sources that a handful of British soldiers got into fistfights with a group of Bostonians at a ropewalk earlier that day (the soldiers were "moonlighting" at the ropewalk).

At around seven that evening, a Boston crowd, or mob, gathered around the customs house to taunt the one soldier on guard at the front door. After they hurled insults, as well as snowballs, he rang a bell that summoned his captain, Thomas Preston, and six other British soldiers. In the confusion that followed, it was hard to say whether the Americans or the British were out of line, or order, but at some point one or two of the British soldiers believed their captain shouted to them to fire, and they did so. Soon the others joined them, and when the smoke cleared there were five Bostonians dead or dying in the snow.

TROOPS DEPART

Virtually all sources agree that acting governor Thomas Hutchinson played a noble role on the night of March 5–6, 1770. He rushed to the customs house, practically threw himself between the British soldiers and the Boston crowd, and prevented a bad situation from becoming much worse. There were moments that night when the Boston crowd might have torn the soldiers limb from limb, and other moments when the British troops might have fired into the crowd, causing much greater casualty numbers. By about five in the morning, everyone was so weary that they went home to bed.

At about eleven that morning, the leaders of Boston's town government—including the ubiquitous Samuel Adams—were at Governor Hutchinson's door, demanding that he remove the two British regiments from the town. Hutchinson held out as long as he could, insisting that he was the civil governor and could not command the military, but when he suggested, as a compromise, that one regiment be removed, Samuel Adams and the other Boston leaders immediately insisted that both must depart. Hutchinson finally gave in, and practically all the red-coated British soldiers went to the islands of Boston Harbor to spend the winter.

THE ADAMS COUSINS

Historians agree on the importance of Samuel Adams to the beginning of the American Revolution, and to the importance of John Adams once that movement was under way, but almost no historian, journalist, or even family member has been able to nail down the links that existed, or how the cause of one led to the other.

Samuel Adams (1722–1803) was born in Boston, where his father and grandfather had achieved a modicum of success in the merchant trade. The millions of beer bottles with Samuel Adams's image on them proclaim his connection to the industry; both his father and he ran a malt brewery in the backyard of the family home. Unlike his ancestors, Samuel Adams was a rather poor man of business. He was much more successful as a politician, first in the Boston town meetings, and then with the Sons of Liberty.

John Adams (1735–1826) was born in Braintree. Like his second cousin, Samuel Adams, John Adams went to Harvard College. Unlike his cousin, John Adams prospered, rising in the practice of the law, and by 1770, the year of the Boston Massacre, he was a prominent attorney in the town. Perhaps he was not as die-hard a patriot as his cousin (not yet, anyhow), but

FOUR OUT OF FIVE

By an odd coincidence, the British government took up an important discussion of American affairs on the same day as the Boston Massacre. Of course, the members of the House of Commons did not know what would happen later that day, 3,000 miles away, but their actions had some bearing on the events that followed.

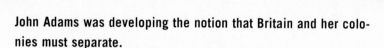

John Adams was developing the notion that Britain and her colonies must separate.

By 1773, the year of the Tea Party, Samuel Adams was the undisputed leader of the Boston crowd, or mob, depending on one's point of view. He was able to call the Boston Town Meetings that threatened the destruction of the tea, and he was able to summon the Sons of Liberty—and allied groups—that carried out the act. No one was prouder than his second cousin, who wrote that the Tea Party was the grandest, boldest act of the decade.

In 1774, Samuel Adams was still the leader of the Adams clan, but when he and his cousin John went to the First Continental Congress in Philadelphia, some observers saw the two cousins as equal in political influence. From that time forward, John Adams became the more public, the more noticed of the two, and his cousin's fame receded as John's advanced. No one ever suggested that the two were rivals (they were too close in many things, including their views on independence). It is interesting, nevertheless, to see how one cousin became the "incendiary," or firebrand, that sparked the American Revolution, while the other became a steady flame that carried it to a successful conclusion.

Prime Minister Lord North rose in the House of Commons to propose that four out of the five Townshend Revenue Acts—those on paper, paint, glass, and lead—be removed while one—the three-penny duty on each pound of tea—remain. Several members of the House of Commons rose to voice their displeasure with Lord North's inconsistency; if he could remove four acts, why not take away all five? But the prime minister made it quite plain that King George would not allow this; there had to be *some* check, some restraint on the American colonists. The impetus for removing the acts was the same as had impelled Britain concerning the Stamp Act: British merchants were losing trade, and therefore money, because of the nonimportation movement in the colonies.

Lord North had his way. The House of Commons removed four out of five Townshend Acts. Just six weeks later, Lord North and the government learned of the Boston Massacre. Now the opponents truly had a field day.

One of the sharpest critics of the Lord North ministry, Edmund Burke, rose in the House of Commons to condemn the policy toward America. "With regard to America. It is time to look for something or other to redress. We have not governed America. We do not govern America. The troops are made prisoners of war [on the islands of Boston Harbor]. You have lost 700,000 pounds in the last year of trade. Natural interest speaks more than a thousand mouths."[4]

Not all members of the House of Commons agreed. There were plenty that believed that Britain could, and did, still govern the colonies. But when Edmund Burke spoke of "natural interest" he struck a strong chord, for members of the House of Commons were naturally sensitive to merchant interests, and the fact that the nonimportation movement had caused a loss of 700,000 pounds sterling was quite serious.

For the moment, neither the House of Commons nor King George could do much about the American colonies. They had to wait to see what unfolded from the Boston Massacre.

TO THE RESCUE

In the spring of 1770, it was decided that there would be a trial of Captain Thomas Preston and his men, but that it would be delayed until the autumn, so that tempers would have a chance to cool down. When it was discovered that neither Captain Preston nor his men could afford attorneys, two prominent Boston patriots stepped forward. John Adams and Josiah Quincy volunteered to serve as defense counsel, free of charge.

Adams and Quincy both believed that the colonies must one day become free of Britain, but they wished to uphold the concept of Anglo-Saxon law that no person should be denied the benefit of legal counsel. They prepared their arguments well, and in November—eight months after the event—they defended Captain Preston and his men in the two cases, *Rex versus Preston* and *Rex versus Weems*.

Defending Captain Preston was easier than defending his men, because Captain Preston was one person, and he was not charged with killing but with having ordered the killing that night. Adams and Quincy won an acquittal for the captain.

Defending the seven British soldiers was more difficult and complex because there was disagreement over who had fired first, and for what reason. Adams and Quincy did their best to make the Boston Massacre seem like a perfectly natural case of self-defense. At a crucial point in the trial, John Adams took some undisguised shots at the Boston crowd, or mob, and his words have been used ever since both for praising the Boston crowd and for denigrating it. "We have been entertained," he began, "with a great variety of phrases, to avoid calling this sort of people a mob—Some call them shavers, some call them geniuses. The plain English is gentlemen, most probably a motley rabble of saucy boys, negroes and mulattoes, Irish teagues and outlandish Jack Tars—And why we should scruple to call such a set of people a mob, I can't conceive, unless the name is too respectable for them."[5]

No one in the courtroom called attention to the fact, but a collection of boys, African Americans, Irishmen, and outlandish

John Adams, a Boston lawyer, offered his legal services to the British soldiers involved in the Boston Massacre because he believed in their right to counsel. After the trial, Adams continued to be involved in colonial matters. Among other achievements, he signed the Declaration of Independence and became the second president of the United States.

sailors pretty much described the Boston Sons of Liberty—the very kind of men John Adams's cousin Samuel used to such great effect in combating British rule. Adams went on to point out the malignant qualities associated with military occupation.

The sun is not about to stand still or go out, nor the rivers to dry up because there was such a mob in Boston on the 5th of March that attacked a party of soldiers. Such things are not new in the world, nor in the British dominions, though they are comparatively, rarities and novelties in this town. . . . [F]rom the nature of things, soldiers quartered in a populous town, will always occasion two mobs, where they prevent one. They are wretched conservators of the peace![6]

Adams and Quincy did very well. Five of the British soldiers were acquitted and two others were found guilty of manslaughter, not murder. Their punishment was to be branded on the thumbs.

PERIOD OF CALM

Remarkably, the Boston Massacre trial appeared to settle the matter. Firebrands like Samuel Adams and James Warren promoted anniversaries of the terrible event of March 5, but the Boston public seemed ready to let the matter go. A relative calm settled over British-American relations for the next year and a half.

Part of the reason was that the nonimportation movement had lost its strength. Even before the king and Parliament removed four out of five Townshend Acts, the nonimportation movement had flagged, partly because so many Americans *did* want to purchase British goods. Once they learned there was only one Townshend Act still in force—the three-penny tax per pound of tea—Bostonians, indeed Americans, went back to buying British merchandise.

In 1771 and the first half of 1772, royal governors, from New Hampshire to Georgia, remarked on the calm state of relations between the colonies and the motherland. One thing that made this calm possible, however, was the continued American success in smuggling.

Even before the Townshend Acts and the nonimportation movement, American colonists had been pleased to buy merchandise from the Dutch, French, or Spaniards, if by so doing they could avoid customs duties. The Dutch colonies in the Caribbean, especially the island of Saint Eustacius, provided many articles for the American colonists, especially tea.

Americans had not ceased drinking tea, but they did buy as little British-imported tea as possible. The Dutch smugglers, and their American counterparts, were very successful in getting ships up to Long Island, and then moving the tea overland to Boston, Newport, or New York. British customs officials estimated that the crown was being denied thousands of pounds of legitimate income each year. So when the calm in colonial relations was broken, it came as the result of an overly zealous British officer trying to do what so many customs officials had attempted: to get Americans to pay what they owed on articles coming from overseas.

The Tea Act

William Dudingston was a lieutenant in King George's navy, and a rather eager, ambitious one at that. In 1768, at the height of the nonimportation movement, he was sent to America to command HMS *Gaspee*, a small cutter intended to police the waters of Delaware Bay.

GASPEE AFFAIR

Dudingston was an efficient officer, who intercepted many American vessels, but he was often outfoxed by the merchant captains who had already brought their smuggled goods ashore. He sometimes used high-handed methods (perhaps out of exasperation) and he earned a bad name among the American skippers and sailors of Delaware Bay. Then, in 1771, he was transferred to the Rhode Island station, to perform customs work in Narragansett Bay.

Rhode Island had a big name among British customs officials as an area that specialized in smuggling. This was because of geography. Thanks to its midway location between Boston and Manhattan, Rhode Island could bring in smuggled articles and send them to either town. Lieutenant Dudingston did his best to clamp down on the smugglers in Narragansett Bay, but he may have gone too far. Both the lieutenant and his vessel became hated symbols of what some Rhode Islanders called British tyranny, and in the summer of 1772, the people of Providence struck back.

On June 9, 1772, John Brown, a prominent merchant of Providence, noticed that the *Gaspee* was chasing him. Knowing the waters extremely well, he made a quick tack to safety and saw with great satisfaction that the *Gaspee* had run aground on the sandbar he had managed to avoid. John Brown went straight to Providence, told the locals that the *Gaspee* was stranded, and within hours he had a posse of citizens, ready to strike a blow.

Sixty men rowed eight longboats that evening, and at about half past midnight, they came within sight of the 70-foot schooner. Someone from the *Gaspee* hailed the longboats, and then Lieutenant Dudingston rose above the bulwark to shout a challenge. He was met by a musket or pistol shot (no one knows which) that hit him somewhere in the groin. Minutes later, the Rhode Islanders swarmed over the ship, which had surrendered. No one else was harmed that night, but the sight of their commander lying in a pool of blood was enough to convince the British to offer no opposition.

Hours later, the Rhode Islanders put Lieutenant Dudingston and his men ashore. By then, the *Gaspee* had burned to the waterline. Whether the Rhode Island men had done this deliberately, or whether it began as the result of a spilled or knocked-over lantern is not known, but the result was the same. One of His Majesty's armed ships had been captured and destroyed by a group of American colonists.

When the HMS *Gaspee* ran aground on a sandbar while chasing smugglers in Narragansett Bay, local citizens piled into boats and attacked the ship and its crew. Lieutenant Dudingston, the commander of the *Gaspee*, was shot and the colonists burned his ship.

Lieutenant Dudingston took the news of the event to Boston and then to London (he recovered from his wound and eventually became an admiral in the British navy). Within two months, the entire British government, and the British public, knew that the Americans had gone farther than ever in their resistance to the king's laws.

CHANGE IN ADMINISTRATION

One reason that punishment was not swifter is that there was a change of administration in London. Lord Hillsborough (to whom Paul Revere had sarcastically dedicated one of his prints) was replaced, in 1772, by Lord Dartmouth, for whom the New Hampshire university is named. A devout Methodist and a calm man much given to deliberation, Dartmouth seemed an immense improvement on Hillsborough, and many colonial agents in London (Benjamin Franklin among them) hoped that British-American relations would now improve for the better. A commission was appointed to examine the *Gaspee* Affair, but after several months of inquiry, its members could obtain nothing more than the testimony of a free African American that some members of Providence's merchant community had been involved. Eventually, the commission decided it was impossible to prosecute anyone for this crime, which took place under the cover of darkness.

As 1772 yielded to 1773, there was still some hope for good relations between the motherland and the colonies. The revelation of a handful of confidential letters, however, soon removed even that faint hope.

HUTCHINSON LETTERS

Thomas Hutchinson was now the full (no longer the acting) governor of Massachusetts. In many ways he seemed an ideal choice.

Born in Boston in 1711, Hutchinson was a fourth-generation American (his great-grandmother, Anne Hutchinson, was a religious rebel who had been cast out of Boston for her nonconformity to Puritan ways). Like Samuel and John Adams, Hutchinson was a graduate of Harvard College and a great lover of his "country," which, to him, meant the Province of Massachusetts Bay. The great difference between Loyalist Thomas Hutchinson and his patriot acquaintances was that he believed British rule was an absolute good, the best that could be found, and he abhorred the violent methods of the Sons of Liberty. He had good reason; the Sons of Liberty had despoiled his in-town mansion in August 1765.

When he became full governor (in 1771), Hutchinson had a brief honeymoon period, during which it seemed he might tread the narrow line between patriot and Loyalist, but in the spring of 1773, a packet of his letters (written in 1768 and 1769) somehow found their way into the hands of Benjamin Franklin, then serving as Massachusetts' agent to London. Franklin sent the letters to his friends in Boston, asking them not to publish them, but knowing full well that they might. The Massachusetts House of Representatives took several weeks to examine the letters and castigate Governor Hutchinson for what they contained, but the full impact was felt when the letters were released and printed by two well-known patriots, Gill and Benjamin Edes, the editors of the *Boston Gazette and Country Journal*. The key, sinister words were found on page 16 of the newspaper:

> This is most certainly a crisis. I really wish that there may not have been the least degree of severity beyond what is absolutely necessary to maintain, I think I may say to you the dependence which a colony ought to have upon the parent state; but if no measures shall have been taken to secure this dependence, or nothing more than some declaratory acts or resolves, *it is all over with us* [emphasis in the original]. The friends of government will be utterly disheartened, and the friends of anarchy will be afraid of nothing.[1]

So far, this did not seem that bad. But in the next paragraph, Hutchinson went farther, to say:

> *There must be an abridgment of what are called English liberties* [emphasis added] I relieve myself by considering that in a remove from the state of nature to the most perfect state of government there must be a great restraint of natural liberty. I doubt whether it is possible to project a system of government in which a colony 3000 miles distant from the parent state shall enjoy all the liberty of the parent state.[2]

Bostonians found this insidious. The key, offending passage was that which spoke of an "abridgment of what are called English liberties." Bostonians believed this was a recipe for tyranny. Even though Thomas Hutchinson had written these letters back in 1769, when he was lieutenant governor, rather than full governor of the province, the Massachusetts House of Representatives impeached Hutchinson and his lieutenant governor, asking that both be removed from Massachusetts government.

Things hung in the balance, with neither side prevailing, until Bostonians, and their fellow Americans, learned that

THE HUTCHINSON-CLARKE CLAN

Governor Thomas Hutchinson was the leader of a large extended family, the tentacles of which ran through the government of Massachusetts and the economy of Boston.

His two eldest sons, Thomas junior and Peter, ran an import firm called Hutchinson & Sons. The two "boys," as Bostonians called them, had been among the last to give up the importation of tea; they had managed to sell it as late as the spring of 1770.

Governor Hutchinson's son-in-law, Andrew Oliver, was the lieutenant governor of the province, and he had been the hated Stamp Act collector whom the Sons of Liberty had forced to resign his post, back in 1765. Richard Clarke, one of the major merchants of Boston, was a cousin of Governor Hutchinson, and the two were neighbors on Beacon Hill.

A good deal is known of the extended Hutchinson clan and their Loyalist allies, because of the many portraits painted by John Singleton Copley (for whom Copley Square is named). He was a son-in-law of Richard Clarke, and he painted many of the prominent Boston Loyalists between about 1765 and 1775. To be fair, he the British government had passed legislation to benefit the East India Company, and that there were ramifications for American consumers.

THE COMPANY

In 1773, the East India Company was about as important to the British economy as General Motors was to the American economy of the 1950s and 1960s. The East India Company (hereafter called simply "the Company") employed thousands of men

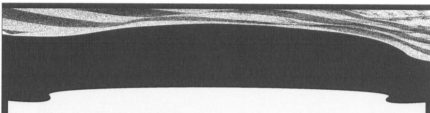

also executed monumental paintings of Boston patriots like Samuel Adams and John Hancock.

Through the Copley portraits, we can see the features and discern the attitudes of the leading Boston Loyalists. They tended to be handsome men and rather beautiful women, with fine features and discriminating faces, but there is also an oblivious quality to them: One senses they did not understand the social change that went on in their midst.

Governor Hutchinson was proud of his large family, and he, they, and many of their relatives moved to London when the American Revolution began. They attempted to live a life akin to what they had experienced before the tumultuous events of the 1770s, but most of them admitted that London—for all its vastness and opulence—was neither as much fun nor as friendly as Boston in previous days. For this, among other reasons, Thomas Hutchinson's most sympathetic biographer entitled his book *The Ordeal of Thomas Hutchinson.*

Baily, Bernard, *The Ordeal of Thomas Hutchinson.* Cambridge, Mass.: Harvard University Press, 1974.

The East India Company was responsible for shipping goods, such as tea and china, throughout the British Empire. The Company was one of the largest businesses in the world and operated a wharf (*above*) in London that employed hundreds of people.

at its docks and warehouses in London and thousands more on the ships that brought articles all the way from China and Sumatra. Thousands of others were employed in the making of Staffordshire pottery, a household industry that produced the cups, saucers, and kettles needed to hold the tea that was served in British homes. By 1773, tea was a very big business and the Company had practically a monopoly.

The Company had not suffered much from the American nonimportation movement, because its biggest customers were in England, but the Company directors did desire to expand into the colonies and to beat the smugglers, who had taken away so much in the way of profits. The Company was developing plans along this line, when, in June 1772, there was a serious financial panic in London that resulted in the failure of nearly a dozen banking and financial houses. Though the Company had not participated in the financial crash, it suffered, like all other merchant houses, and toward the end of 1772 it seemed as if the great East India Company might go under.

Everyone understood that this could not be allowed to happen.

GOVERNMENT INTERVENTION

In the winter of 1772–1773, Lord North and his government took steps to save the East India Company. They found that the Company board of directors had been downright negligent, paying out far too much in dividends to stockholders. As a result, the British government took over parts of the Company's operation and put new guidelines on its management. These included the reduction of dividends *and* the reduction of customs duties, so that the Company could expand to new markets.

These moves made sense because the Company had a great backlog of tea (as much as 18 million pounds) in its London warehouses. By reducing the typical customs duties paid on imported tea, and allowing the Company to sell directly to its American customers, the government of Lord

North was creating a win-win-win situation. The Company would survive; the government would not have to fear a major financial collapse in the markets; and the American colonists would receive their tea cheaper than ever before. Lord North did not keep a diary of these actions (nor was America very much on his mind), but one can imagine him congratulating himself for having found a solution that provided something for everyone.

The Tea Act was introduced to the House of Commons in April, and passed in May 1773. There was remarkably little controversy, because everyone saw the need to save the East India Company, but a few members of the House did protest against the retention of the Townshend duty on tea. Back in 1767, the five Townshend Acts had put duties on paper, paint, glass, lead, and tea. Now, only the duty on tea remained.

William Dowdeswell, a regular member of the loyal opposition, rose in the House of Commons to speak against retaining the duty (or tax) on tea. "I observe that the noble lord [Lord North] has made no proposition to the duty laid upon tea imported into America. If the noble lord intends to leave that duty as it is he will not serve the East India Company at all in admitting a drawback to America. . . . I tell the noble lord now, if he doesn't take off the duty, they won't take the tea."[3]

Lord North replied that King George was determined to keep at least one tax, or duty, to show the Americans that the British government was in earnest. Besides, he expressed, how could the Americans complain? They would get their tea cheaper than ever before!

The Tea Act passed on May 10, with a minimum of debate. So obvious did the measure seem that the vote in the House of Commons was not recorded, meaning that it passed by a quick voice vote.

Lord North, King George, and the British government did not realize what a hornet's nest they had stirred.

Town Meetings
and Committees
of Correspondence

The British government approved the Tea Act in May 1773, but most Americans did not receive the news until late summer or even the beginning of autumn. When they did, the response was fast and furious.

PHILADELPHIA

The town of Brotherly Love had been one of the quietest during the Stamp Act, and even the Townshend Revenue Acts had not stirred up much trouble. This was because Philadelphia—which had surpassed Boston as the largest American town—had prospered during the past decade, while its fellow port towns (including Boston and New York) had been mired in an economic recession.

Philadelphians were generally more passive politically than Bostonians or New Yorkers, but the news of the Tea Act sprang many of them into action. Almost at once, it was decided that there should be town meetings and committees chosen to call upon the tea consignees, to make them resign their offices.

CONSIGNEES

The East India Company did not have any offices in the American colonies, so, as soon as the Tea Act was passed, a number

PHILADELPHIA RESOLVES

On October 16, a large crowd (perhaps 8,000 people) gathered at the State House in Philadelphia. After some hours, they decided on the following resolves:

Resolved, That the disposal of their own property is the inherent right of freemen; that there can be no property in which another can, of right, take from us without our consent; that the claim of Parliament to tax America is, in other words, a claim of right to levy contributions on us at pleasure.

That the duty imposed by Parliament upon tea landed in America is a tax on the Americans, or levying contributions on them without their consent.

That the express purpose for which the tax is levied on the Americans, namely for the support of government, administration of justice, and defense of his Majesty's dominions in America, has a direct tendency to render Assemblies useless, and to introduce arbitrary government and slavery.

That a virtuous and steady opposition to this Ministerial plan of governing America is absolutely necessary to preserve even the shadow of liberty, and is a duty which every freeman in America owes to his country, to himself, and to his posterity.

That the resolution lately entered into by the East India Company to send out their tea to America, subject to the pay-of Americans living in London came forward to offer their services—and those of their friends and relatives. A typical letter from a would-be consignee was as follows:

> Honorable Sirs:
>
> We take the liberty of recommending Monsieurs Willing, Morris, and Company of Philadelphia to be your agents

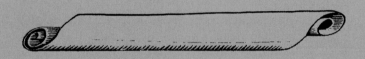

ment of duties on its being landed here, is an open attempt to enforce this Ministerial plan, and a violent attack upon the liberties of America.

That it is the duty of every American to oppose this attempt.

That whoever shall, directly or indirectly, countenance this attempt, or in any wise aid or abet in unloading, receiving, or vending the tea sent to or to be sent out by the East India Company, while it remains subject to the payment of a duty here, is *an enemy of his country* [emphasis added].

That a committee be immediately chosen to wait on those gentlemen who, it is reported, are appointed by the East India Company to receive and sell said tea, and request them, from a regard to their own characters, and the peace and good order of the city and province to resign their appointment.*

Years later, when the State House was renamed the Hall of Independence, and then Independence Hall, Americans looked on this time, in 1773, as among the proudest moments of the patriot cause in Philadelphia.

---

* Etting, Frank M. *An Historical Account of the Old State House of Pennsylvania Now Known as The Hall of Independence.* Boston: James R. Osgood & Company, 1876, pp. 67–68.

there, for any quantity of tea you may please to consign them for sale, and which they will dispose of in the best manner they can for the benefit of the Commissioner on the following terms:

The tea to be sold at two months prompt, to be paid for on delivery, and the money to be paid out at the exchange which shall be current at that time, into the Company's treasury within three months after it is received from Philadelphia. Willing, Morris & Company to be allowed 5 per cent for commission, and 1 per cent for warehouse room and all other charges, except freight and duty.[1]

This basic arrangement was offered to consignees of the tea, and many merchants in the American coastal towns were eager to take the offer. They soon experienced considerable opposition from their countrymen, however.

OPPOSITION GROWS

As details of the Tea Act became known, Americans from Boston to Charles Town, South Carolina, expressed anger over its provisions. True, the Townshend Revenue Act was only a duty of three pence per pound, but many Americans said (and shouted!) that this was the beginning of the road to tyranny, that once Parliament pulled this tax over on the Americans, there would be no stopping.

Some observers at the time, and many historians since, have noted that the resistance was not all noble and high-minded. Quite a few coastal merchants had become wealthy through the smuggling of Dutch imported tea, and their fortunes would take a hit if the East India Company made strong inroads into the American market. Along with the denunciation of the tax on tea, many Americans were furious at the idea that the East India Company had been granted what was, in effect, a monopoly.

Some of the strongest words of protest came from New York. The province was under the rule of Governor William Tryon, widely perceived as one of the most effective and aggressive of

After the Tea Act was passed, colonists began boycotting British products in protest of being taxed without representation in the British Parliament. A group of women in Edenton, South Carolina, were satirized (*above*) for organizing a "tea party," an event where the attendees would sign pledges to not drink British tea or wear British cloth.

the royal governors, and there was a fear that he might use the British navy to cram the tea down American throats. To forestall that possibility, the New York newspapers featured a letter to the editor on November 27, 1773:

> Whereas our Nation have lately been informed that the Fetters which have been forged for us (by the Parliament of Great Britain) are hourly expected to arrive, in a certain ship, belonging to, or chartered by, the East India Company. We do therefore declare, that we are determined not to be enslaved by any power on earth; and that whosoever shall aid or abet so infamous a design, or shall presume to let their store or stores, for the reception of the infernal chains, may depend upon it, that we are prepared, and shall not fail to pay them an unwelcome visit, in which they shall be treated as their deserve, by THE MOHAWKS.[2]

This was, almost certainly, the first time that Native Americans of any type had been invoked in the tea controversy. Doubtless, the letter was written by American colonials, dressed in wool or cotton, and not in deerskin or bearskin, but the poignant words made plain that white American colonials were willing to use native methods to prevent the "infernal chains" from coming to America.

So far, the strongest opposition had been registered in the middle colonies, with Philadelphia and New York leading the way.

BOSTON'S SUMMER

Boston, in the late summer of 1773, was the calmest and quietest it had been for years. Even Governor Hutchinson, who had been impeached by the House of Representatives, remarked that the town was in the best shape he had seen in years. But when news of the Tea Act came—in August and September— the mood shifted very quickly.

Even before they saw the text of the Tea Act, Bostonians realized that the Townshend duty would still be in place. No matter that they would be able to purchase tea cheaply; they were dead set against the beverage, which people began to call the odious drink. Some of the most negative feelings were voiced against Richard Clarke and Sons and the two Hutchinson sons. Ann Hulton—sister of the British revenue commissioner in Boston—had this to say to her London correspondent:

> The ships laden with tea from the East India House are hourly expected, the people will not suffer it to be landed at Boston, they demand the consignees to promise to send it back. Mr. Clark resolutely refuses to comply, will submit to no other terms, than to put it into warehouse till they can hear from England. They threaten to tear him to pieces if it's landed, he says he will be torn to pieces before he will desert the trust reposed in him by the consigners.[3]

Richard Clark had long endured the fury of the Boston crowd, which he returned with a consummate scorn. The painting executed of him by his son-in-law, Jonathan Copley, shows steely blue eyes and a distant expression—the kind one expects of a man who has had his way in life, and who will not submit to the demands of a rabble. Even so, Clark, his immediate family, and some of their friends were so threatened by a group of Bostonians (on November 1) that they fled to Castle William for safety, where they were joined by a number of other tea consignees. Boston was behind Philadelphia and New York in demonstrating its indignation, but it was making up for lost time.

CHARLES TOWN

The Southern colonies were a bit behind their northern brethren, but they, too, decided to make up for lost time. Josiah Martin, the royal governor of North Carolina, wrote to Lord Dartmouth, secretary of state for the colonies, in mid-December:

ADVERTISEMENT.

THE Members of the Affociation of the Sons of Liberty, are requefted to meet at the City-Hall, at one o'Clock, To-morrow, (being Friday) on Bufi-nefs of the utmoft Importance ;—And every other Friend to the Liberties, and Trade of America, are hereby moft cordially invited, to meet at the fame Time and Place.   *The Committee of the Affociation.*

Thurfday, NEW-YORK, 16th December, 1773.

Samuel Adams organized meetings for the Committees of Correspondence and the Sons of Liberty through newspaper advertisements. These meetings were held throughout the colonies and allowed people to discuss the impact of British legislation on the colonies and the long-term effects they were to have on local economies and governments.

My Lord . . . The spirit of the Assembly contains expressions so unfit, and breathes a spirit so unbecoming a people living under the mild and just government of His Majesty, that it gives me pain to lay it before your lordship; and I transmit with no less concern a copy of certain resolves entered upon the journals of that House which display like discontent and disrespect to government.[4]

North Carolinians were not that concerned about tea—none was slated for their docks—but they had a set of grievances they wanted addressed, and, given the temper of the time, it is quite likely that they did show disrespect both to the governor and the king. Their South Carolina neighbors were equally up in arms. Lieutenant Governor William Bull wrote to the Earl of Dartmouth late in the year that

> Captain Curling arrived here with 257 chests of tea sent by the East India Company with the same instructions to agents appointed here as at Boston, New York, and Philadelphia. The spirit which had been raised in those towns with great threats of violence to hinder the landing and disposing of the tea there was communicated to this province by letters, Gazettes and merchants.[5]

About the only source that Governor Bull did *not* cite was the committees of correspondence, which had sprung into action over the previous 12 months.

COMMITTEES

Samuel Adams had proposed a series of committees of correspondence in the autumn of 1772. He did so in response to rumors that the Townshend revenue was to be used to pay the salaries of governors throughout the colonies, thus making them less dependent on the colonial legislatures.

The committees of correspondence had been a major success, bigger than Samuel Adams ever expected. At first they were almost all in Massachusetts towns, then in New England towns, but by the autumn of 1773, the idea had spread to all parts of the colonies except Georgia, which, as the most recently settled, had stronger ties to the Crown than to its fellow colonies. The committees of correspondence moved information about the Tea Act—and its possible implications—to virtually all parts of British America.

The Governor,
the Rabble,
and the Rebels

G overnor Thomas Hutchinson had endured many pains
and disappointments during his tenure in office. He
was greatly offended that his fellow Massachusetts citizens
did not understand that he worked for their good, and that
he believed British government to be the best that could be
found anywhere in the world. On previous occasions, such as
the removal of British soldiers from the town after the Boston
Massacre, Governor Hutchinson had shown himself to be
reasonable and willing to compromise, but in November and
December 1773 he held what he considered a winning hand.
If the Bostonians were foolish enough to refuse the East India
Company tea, the governor could seize it, and eventually
push it down the mouths of the recalcitrant people of Boston
and Massachusetts.

THE LAW

Customs law in America depended on the Navigation Acts of the 1660s, one of which explicitly declared that a vessel and its cargo could be seized if the duties were not paid within 20 days of its arrival. A countdown therefore began on November 28, when the *Dartmouth* came to anchor in King's Road.

For once, Governor Hutchinson had the full weight of the royal power behind him. Not only did British ships surround the *Dartmouth*—and those that came later—but there were hundreds of marines aboard those ships, men perfectly capable of bringing a cargo to land, whether by peaceful means or by force. Hutchinson was all too aware that Samuel Adams and the Sons of Liberty would oppose any landing; the question was what the more sober and traditional folk of Boston would do.

TOWN MEETING

Boston had a long tradition of town meetings, usually held in the first week of May to determine the annual budget, but in November and December 1773 a number of extraordinary meetings were held, and people were invited to come from neighboring towns as well. Governor Hutchinson saw this as a flagrant violation of the law, but he was unable to prevent the Bostonians, and their countryside cousins, from meeting. To do so, Hutchinson would need the unanimous agreement of his governor's council, and those that came at his summons showed no desire to alienate the Boston crowd. To Hutchinson, it was an old story; the defenders of the king's interest spoke loudly when nothing was at stake, and ran like frightened rabbits in any time of crisis.

Samuel Adams and his friends had a legalistic way out of the situation; they called the town meetings "assemblies of the public" to defy the regular rules of engagement. This infuriated Governor Hutchinson, who gathered the governor's council—a body of about 20 leading men of the colony—

only to find that a majority of its members sympathized with the patriots, at least over the matter of tea. The first tea ship arrived in late December.

LOG OF THE *DARTMOUTH*

Though she carried Chinese tea all the way from England, and though she had been sent by the British East India Company, the *Dartmouth* was actually American owned. She belonged to Francis Rotch, the wealthiest merchant on Nantucket, who, a few years earlier, had fought a no-holds-barred trade war with the patriot merchant John Hancock over the merchandizing of whale oil. Francis Rotch prevailed on that occasion, and the rivalry of the House of Rotch and the House of Hancock (as they were called) played a part, however small, in increasing the stakes in this situation. The ship's log of the *Dartmouth* reveals the methods one took in entering Boston Harbor:

> Sunday, November 28. This 24 hours first part fresh breezes, hazy weather, with rain at times. At sunset [we] fetched in with the *Graves*, tacked to the southward. At 10 P.M., [we] came to anchor about two miles above the Light House, got our boat out, and went on shore for the pilot.[1]

This "Light House" was Boston Light, on Little Brewster Island, which is today the oldest lighthouse in continuous operation in the United States. Captain Bruce Hall brought a local pilot aboard from the island and threaded his way in cautiously, past the many isles and shoals of the harbor:

> At 11, the tide being ebb, [we] got under way, and turned up and came to anchor under the Admiral's stern. At 10 at night, two custom-house officers were boarded upon us by the Castle, we being the first ship ever boarded in this manner, which happened on account of our having the East India Company's *accursed dutiable tea* on board [emphasis in the original].[2]

Discussion of the Tea Act became more intense as the *Dartmouth* pulled into Boston Harbor. This American-owned ship was filled with British tea and imports, and the American colonists held a massive meeting to decide what to do with the vessel's cargo and owner.

The "Castle" was Castle William, to which most of the tea consignees had fled during the past 10 days, as it was the only sure place of refuge at a time when tempers were hot in the town. The "admiral's stern" referred to the flagship of Admiral John Montagu, who commanded the ships, the marines, and the cannon intended to guard the tea, and if necessary to ensure that it was landed.

TOWN MEETING

The *Dartmouth*'s arrival threw the town into a commotion. If the earlier town meetings—disguised as meetings of the whole body of the people—had been large, then the one held on the last day of November and the first of December was, quite possibly, the largest ever seen in Boston, perhaps in all New England.

The meeting came to order in Faneuil Hall, but the number of persons was so great that it was adjourned to meet at the Old South Meeting House, in what is now the South End of Boston. Though Samuel Adams was the guiding spirit of the meeting, Jonathan Williams was chosen moderator, meaning that he would direct the tone and direction of the debates.

The first measure proposed was that the town should consider the cargo of the *Dartmouth* a pernicious invasion by the British ministry, and that it should be "returned to the place from whence it came at all events."[3] This passed by unanimous decision. A message was then sent to the tea consignees—Messieurs Faneuil, Clark, Hutchinson, and Winslow—demanding them to answer whether they would send the tea back to England. The meeting was adjourned until three in the afternoon, so that the consignees might have time to answer.

When the large crowd—estimated at between 4,000 and 6,000 persons—returned, Francis Rotch, the Nantucket merchant who owned the *Dartmouth*, stood before the meeting to register a protest against its actions. He was simply a merchant, trying to sell wares his captain had obtained in England. The town meeting heard him out, then voted that Captain Bruce Hall be warned "at his peril he is not to suffer any of the tea brought by him to be landed."[4] Another vote was taken to the effect that a permanent guard of volunteers should be placed aboard the *Dartmouth*, to prevent the tea from being brought ashore, or any violence being done to the captain and crew. Captain Edward Procter of the town militia was given command of the first night's watch. The meeting then adjourned.

What Governor Hutchinson thought of this can only be imagined. He was the leading government official in the town, and he had the Royal Navy behind him, yet here was Samuel Adams acting as if the Boston Town Meeting—practically an illegal body at that time—was the real government of Boston. When the town meeting came to order again on November 30, Sheriff Greenleaf arrived with a summons from the governor, ordering the town meeting to cease and desist, and for the people to return home. The summons was read aloud, but all that the men assembled would give by way of answer was

THE NEW ENGLAND TOWN MEETING

The Puritans who settled at Salem in 1629 and at Boston in 1630 very quickly established the concept that adult, free-holding males (those who owned property free and clear) should come together, on as many occasions as necessary, to vote in select men, clerks, assistants, and—at least in some towns—chimney sweeps! For the first 50 years of its existence, Boston—and the entire colony of Massachusetts Bay—had employed this practice of local self-government. Then, in 1686, a new royal governor, Sir Edmund Andros, appeared; he demanded that the towns (Boston and all the rest) restrict themselves to only one town meeting a year, preferably to be held in the first week of May.

Sir Edmund Andros was overthrown in a bloodless, one-day coup in April 1689, and the people of Massachusetts had earnestly sought restoration of their earlier rights. Under the new charter of the province, which arrived in 1692, the people of Boston, and Massachusetts, had the right to assemble as often as they pleased, but they could only do so in their local communities (according to this proviso, the special town meetings of November and December were illegal because they brought in so many people from other communities).

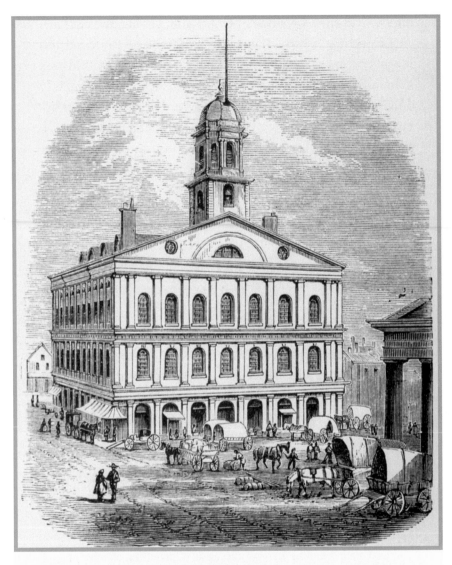

Unauthorized meetings were illegal, but Samuel Adams frequently organized events during which people could discuss the issues that affected the colonies. After the controversial arrival of the *Dartmouth*, the usual meeting in Faneuil Hall (*above*), ballooned to approximately 6,000 people in attendance and had to be moved to the Old South Meeting Hall.

"a loud and very general hiss."[5] Some reports have Samuel Adams standing at that moment to make a personal attack on Governor Hutchinson:

"To Hutchinson's description of himself as 'his Majesty's Representative in this province,' Adams replied, 'He? He? Is he that shadow of a man, scarce able to support his withered carcass or his hoary head? Is he a representation of majesty?'"[6] The irony was not lost on his listeners. Whatever they thought of Governor Hutchinson, everyone admitted he was the picture of elegant, slim health, while Samuel Adams, a full decade younger was pale faced, slightly overweight, and had a bad case of palsy, which gave him a tremor in the hands.

After a chorus of chortles—both over the governor's demand and Adams's response—the town meeting voted not to disperse. The crisis was at a boiling point, when Jonathan Copley—the best portrait painter in town and the son-in-law of tea merchant Richard Clarke—stood to offer his services. He would go to Castle William, he said, to obtain a firm answer from them on whether to return the tea to England. As the in-law of several of the consignees and as the son of poor parents who had migrated from Ireland in the 1730s, Copley was in a rather unusual position: He could speak to both sides of the argument without offending either. Therefore, the town meeting adjourned for several hours to let Copley speak to his relatives on Castle Island. He returned at two in the afternoon and "acquainted the body that he had seen all the consignees"[7] and that their response was that it would do no good for them to appear before the town meeting. This was voted as completely unsatisfactory. Only a little business remained. The town meeting voted the volunteer guard to stand on the *Dartmouth* that evening, and a vote of thanks was given to "those of this body . . . who have come from the neighboring towns, for their countenance and union."[8]

Days passed without an incident.

MORE SHIPS

The *Beaver* and the *Eleanor* arrived about ten days after the *Dartmouth*. Both were small vessels (neither carried as much tea as the *Dartmouth*), but there were now three ships bearing the hated East India Company product. By now, Samuel Adams and the town meeting participants had prevailed upon Francis Rotch and Captain Bruce Hall to bring the *Dartmouth* to Griffin's Wharf on the south side of town where there was less protection from His Majesty's naval forces. The *Beaver* and the *Eleanor* joined them and a standoff followed, with Governor Hutchinson insisting that the ships must unload their cargoes and the people of Boston, at least those that dared to speak on the matter, saying they must not.

News of the Boston standoff spread to other towns and other colonies, and by mid-December the people of New York and Philadelphia knew that the Bostonians were now at the epicenter of the great controversy. The royal governor in Charles Town had already brought the tea destined for that town ashore and put it under lock and key. The royal governor of New York had not been forced to the point, because the tea ship destined for that town was late in arrival. Everything, it appeared, depended on Boston.

THE LAST MEETING

Early in the morning on December 14, a handbill appeared on the streets of Boston:

"Friends! Brethren! Countrymen! The perfidious act of your reckless enemies to render ineffectual the late resolves of the body of the people, demands your assembling at the Old South Meeting House, precisely at ten o'clock this day, at which time the bells will ring."[9]

At nine in the morning on December 16, 1773, the Boston town meeting met once more. Everyone there (the crowd was estimated at about 6,000) knew this was the last time, for the 20-day deadline would be passed at midnight; under British naval law, goods on which the king's duty was not paid within 20 days were liable to seizure. No one knew whether Governor Hutchinson intended to act at midnight or to wait until morning, but he would have the upper hand because he could use the full might of the Royal Navy against the town (whether he *wanted* to was unlikely).

The mood of the meeting was somber. The majority of Bostonians believed that the imposition of a tea duty—in this case—was tantamount to tyranny, and that it would be a sign for King George and Parliament to impose all sorts of new taxes on the colonies. Having heard the news from New York and Philadelphia, Bostonians knew that they were at the center of the storm.

A few last efforts were made. Francis Rotch came to the meeting to appeal for the safety of his ship and its merchandise. Samuel Adams and other leaders of the meeting told him, rather sternly, to move the *Dartmouth* out of harm's way by sending it back to England. That he could not do, Rotch answered, for once a ship had come to port she must unload her merchandise before departing; if he attempted to leave, the Royal Navy ships might well fire (as might the cannon at Castle William). Francis Rotch made one last appeal: Would the town meeting wait while he went to see Governor Hutchinson in person? This was agreed, and the town meeting adjourned for several hours. When it came back into session, at four in the afternoon, it was nearly dark and candles were lit in the Old South Meeting House.

He had appeared at the governor's private home in Milton to make his request, Francis Rotch said, and the answer had been in the negative. Governor Hutchinson would not give him a pass to depart. Either the tea must be unloaded before midnight (almost an impossibility) or the Royal Navy would be sent to seize it.

Samuel Adams had waited a long time for this moment. Like a consummate politician, he knew that he could not move until all the peaceful means had been exhausted. He had laid his plans, his contingencies, and now, on hearing Francis Rotch's answer, Adams rose to say:

"This meeting can do nothing more to save the country!"[10]

The Tea Party

To this day, we do not know if Samuel Adams spoke those ten words out of exasperation out of weariness or with a quiet sense of triumph. They were immediately followed by a handful of others:

"To Griffin's Wharf!"

"Boston Harbor a teapot tonight!"[1]

The Tea Party was on.

TO THE WHARF

The distance from Old South Meeting House to Griffin's Wharf was a ten-minute walk at most, and many of the participants took it at the run. Some, but not all, took time to smear their faces with powder and soot, and some dressed themselves as Native Americans (whether they were Mohawk or Narragansett is difficult to say).

In minutes, the three tea ships were boarded, with the officers and crew making no resistance. The men then proceeded to enter the ship's holds and bring out the many chests of tea (342 in all) that had come from London.

The night was eerily calm and quiet. There had been a light rain earlier, and there was a half-moon that began to rise as the men chopped their way into the chests, then heaved the still half-open chests over the sides of the ships. Because the tide was falling, some of the chests were soon stuck in mud and sand just below the waterline.

The work continued for about three hours, with few sounds other than those made by hatchets. A crowd of about a thousand people—men, women, and children—gathered in the vicinity to observe the action. There were plenty of Royal Navy marines just a few hundred yards away, but no one made a move to protect the tea.

No one knows just how many persons were involved in the hatchet strokes or the dropping of tea over the side (estimates run from as few as 40 to as many as 150). What can be said with certainty is that the majority of Bostonians were in favor of the action: No one appeared to speak against it or to lift a hand against the perpetrators. The tension that had built for the previous two months finally exploded into one major scene of action, and most Bostonians applauded.

HEADING HOME

Within three hours, all the work was done. Three hundred and forty-two chests of tea had been dumped over the side, and an awful mess had been created because of the low tide. George R.T. Hewes later described how one of his fellows tried to make off with some of the tea:

> [He] filled his pockets, and also the lining of his coat. But I had detected him, and gave information to the captain of

(continues on page 62)

The eyewitness account of George Robert Twelve Hewes was taken many years later, but it remains one of the best descriptions by any of the participants.

> The meeting was immediately dissolved, many of them crying out, Let every man do his duty, and be true to his country; and there was a general huzza for Griffin's wharf. It was now evening, and I immediately dressed myself in the costume of an Indian, equipped with a small hatchet, which I and my associates denominated the tomahawk, with which, and a club, after having painted my face and hands with coal dust in the shop of a blacksmith, I repaired to Griffin's wharf.*

Hewes does not tell us how he had prepared all this in advance, but one gets the sense that he and his fellows had expected that the town meeting would not solve the situation, and that this desperate action would be called for.

> When we arrived at the wharf, there were three of our number who assumed an authority to direct our operations, to which we readily submitted. They divided us into three parties, for the purpose of boarding the three ships which contained the tea at the same time. The name of him who commanded the division to which I was assigned, was Leonard Pitt.**

Most of the names of the Tea Party men remain in dispute, but we are reasonably confident that Pitt was indeed one of the leaders.

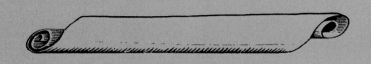

> The commander of the division to which I belonged, as soon
> as we were on board the ship, appointed me boatswain [pro-
> nounced *bo'sun*], and ordered me to go to the captain and
> demand of him the keys to the hatches and a dozen candles.
> I made the demand accordingly, and the captain promptly
> replied and delivered the articles; but requested me at the
> same time to do no damage to the ship or rigging.***

We do not know which of the three ships Hewes boarded, but
by this time all three were swarmed by patriot volunteers, and
there was no resistance, no shots fired in the night.

> We were then ordered by our commander to open the
> hatches, and take out all the chests of tea and throw them
> overboard, and we immediately proceeded to execute his
> orders; first cutting and splitting the chests with our toma-
> hawks, so as thoroughly to expose them to the effects of the
> water.****

George R.T. Hewes makes this sound very easy, but some of
those chests weighed 450 pounds, and they had to be hauled up
from the ship's hold, cut into, and then thrown over the side. This
was an evening of hot work.

---

* *A Retrospect of the Boston Tea Party, with a Memoir of George R.T.
Hewes*, by a citizen of New York. New York: S.S. Bliss Printer, 1834, p. 38.
** Ibid., pp. 38–39.
*** Ibid., p. 39.
**** Ibid.

After hearing Governor Hutchinson's order to either unload the *Dartmouth*'s cargo or have it seized by the Royal Navy, angry colonists dressed as Native Americans, marched to the ship, and heaved chests of tea into Boston Harbor.

(continued from page 59)

what he was doing. We were ordered to take him into custody, and just as he was stepping from the vessel, I seized him by the skirt of his coat, and in attempting to pull him back, I tore it off; but springing forward, by a rapid effort, he made his escape. He had to run a gauntlet through the crowd upon the wharf; each one, as he passed, giving him a kick or a stroke.[2]

This fellow was by no means the only person to sneak off with little bits of tea leaves. Some people managed to secure the tea as a souvenir, and it remained in their families until it was purchased by the Massachusetts Historical Society, which keeps a small bit of it to this day.

As the Tea Party participants left the scene and headed for home, the window of a house fronting on Griffin's Wharf was opened. Rear Admiral John Montagu had come ashore earlier in the day. One reason the British Navy was unable to do anything during the Tea Party was that the commanding officer was not aboard his flagship. Numerous reports of the admiral's words have circulated over the decades, but they were something like the ones that follow.

"Well, boys, you've had a fine, pleasant evening for your Indian caper, haven't you? But mind, you've got to pay the fiddler yet!"[3]

One source has the answer coming from Leonard Pitts, commander of the division to which George R.T. Hewes was assigned:

"Oh, never mind, Squire, Just come out here, if you please, and we'll settle the bill in two minutes."[4]

The window was hastily closed.

The Tea Party, what people called the Destruction of the Tea, was over.

JOHN ADAMS

No one knows if Samuel Adams played any part in the Tea Party itself. He was silent about it for the rest of his life. His cousin, John Adams, definitely did not participate in the action at Griffin's Wharf, but his feeling about it can be seen in his diary entry, on December 17: "This is the most magnificent movement of all. There is a dignity, a majesty, a sublimity in this last effort of the Patriots that I greatly admire. . . . This destruction of the tea is so bold, so daring, so firm, intrepid, & inflexible, and it must have so important consequences and so lasting, that I cannot but consider it an epocha in history."[5]

PAUL REVERE

Sometime the next morning, Paul Revere saddled up his best horse and rode out, carrying reports of what had transpired

Paul Revere was well known for his skilled work as a silversmith, but after the Boston Tea Party, he began working as a dispatch rider for the Committee of Correspondence. Revere was responsible for delivering messages from the Boston meetings to the organization's other chapters in Manhattan and other groups along the way.

and letters from Boston's Committee of Correspondence. He had plenty of places to stop along the way, but his major mission was to reach Manhattan, 170 miles distant.

Revere had been one of the Sons of Liberty from the very beginning, but his days as the all-important dispatch rider had just begun. He was 38 when this job was given to him, and he did not disappoint, covering the miles to New York City in just four days (given the state of the roads and paths at the time, this was a major achievement). New Yorkers were pleased to hear that Boston had acted with such firmness, and the news was sped on to Philadelphia by another rider, for it was time for Paul Revere to get home. A Philadelphia town meeting expressed its sentiments on Monday, December 27:

> The unanimity, spirit, and zeal which have heretofore animated all the colonies, from Boston to South Carolina, have been so eminently displayed in the opposition to the pernicious project of the East India Company . . . that a particular account of the transactions of this city cannot but be acceptable to all our readers, and every other friend of American liberty.[6]

The *Pennsylvania Packet* went on to remind its readers that Philadelphia had voted for the eight resolutions that spoke against the tea and that New York had done likewise, but everyone understood that the greatest praise was for Boston, which had dumped the East India Company tea into the harbor. One thing that neither the Philadelphians nor the Bostonians understood at that moment, was just how personally the British government would take this daring move.

TURNING BACK THE SHIP

Two days earlier, on Christmas Day, a number of patriotic Philadelphians had gone downriver a few miles to meet Captain Ayres, whose ship the *Polly* was bringing tea to their city. Reminding him of the resolutions voted by the town, the Philadelphia leaders were able to persuade Captain Ayres to turn back. There would be no Philadelphia Tea Party.

YEAR'S END

As 1773 came to an end, many American colonists were jubilant over how the tea issue had been settled. They saw the effort to market tea as a nasty scheme cooked up by Lord North and the East India Company; they did not realize that the full faith and power of King George's government had been behind it. Their sense of victory would be short-lived, however. Bostonians had not heard the last about their action.

Boston's Punishment

N ews of the Tea Party reached almost all parts of the colonies within three weeks, but it was twice that long before King George, Lord North, and the House of Commons received the news. All three were appalled.

REPORTS

Ann Hulton wrote to her London correspondent at the end of January 1774: "You will perhaps expect me to give you some account of the state of Boston & late proceedings here but really the times are too bad & the scenes too shocking for me to describe. I suppose you will have heard long before this arrives of the fate of the tea."[1]

Hulton went on to lament the fate of the tea consignees, those who had agreed to handle sales for the East India Company: "The tea consignees remain still at the Castle. Six weeks since the tea was destroyed, and there is no prospect of their ever returning & residing in Boston with safety. This place, & all the towns about entered into a written agreement not to afford them any shelter or protection."2

One of the consignees and his wife had been hounded out of Plymouth, Massachusetts, in the middle of a snowstorm.

THE KING

King George opened Parliament on January 13, 1774. His speech from the throne made only a mention or two of America because London had other concerns at that time. The king made much of the fortunate position that Britain currently enjoyed; she was the predominant power in Europe, yet she had no ambitions, no designs on her neighbors.

THE MINISTRY

The merchant ship *Hayley* brought the news of the Tea Party to London on January 19, and Governor Hutchinson's official report came on January 27. A week later, the cabinet of ministers met at St. James Palace.

Lord North had long been in favor of tougher actions against the Americans, but his hands had been tied, both by members of Parliament who disagreed and by his half brother Lord Dartmouth, secretary of state for the colonies. On this occasion, Lord Dartmouth was very much in step with his half brother; they agreed that it was necessary to strike hard and fast to make the Bostonians regret what they had done. Between them, Lord North and Lord Dartmouth began drawing up Boston's punishment.

DR. FRANKLIN

The first American to feel the rage of the British government and public, was Benjamin Franklin (1706–1790). Born in Boston at the turn of the eighteenth century, Franklin had moved to Philadelphia as a teenager, and the town of Brotherly Love

BENJAMIN FRANKLIN.
THE STATESMAN AND PHILOSOPHER.

Benjamin Franklin, a noted printer, politician, and inventor living in Philadelphia, traveled to England to serve as Pennsylvania's colonial agent. As Pennsylvania's representative, it was Franklin's job to defend the interests and needs of his colony to royal officials in London.

had been his permanent home for many years. During the 1760s, Franklin had gone to London to act as the colonial agent for Pennsylvania, and, sometime over the years, he had become the Massachusetts agent as well. As such, he was a natural target for British anger.

On January 29, 1774, just seven weeks after the Tea Party, Franklin stood, hat in hand, in the "cockpit," the reception chamber of the king's Privy Council. The king's attorney general, Alexander Wedderburn, made Franklin into the great scapegoat for all that had gone astray in British-American relations over the years. Franklin stood in dignified silence, while Wedderburn attacked him for

☆ releasing the private correspondence of Thomas Hutchinson to the public,
☆ encouraging his Massachusetts constituents to resist the rule of George III,
☆ helping to bring about the impeachment of Hutchinson and Andrew Oliver.

Franklin chose not to answer the charges, but it has often been claimed that he turned to a British bureaucrat later and said he would make George III into a little king for this public humiliation. This was only the beginning, however.

PARLIAMENT

At the beginning of the parliamentary session, the American colonies were not much on the minds of Lord North or the members of the House of Commons, but that changed as information about the Tea Party came in. When first they heard of it, most British leaders (even those who had long been sympathetic to America) branded it an act of flagrant disregard for property. At the very least, the Americans must pay for what they had destroyed.

Prime Minister Lord North finally had the free hand he had so long desired. Ever since coming to the ministry in 1770, he had looked for a way to strike back at the colonies that showed such disrespect for king, Parliament, and all of Great Britain.

Beginning in February, he laid American affairs on the table (literally) by presenting reports of the Tea Party and quotations from American newspapers. The colonies still had friends in the House of Commons—notably Edmund Burke, William Dowdeswell, and Isaac Barre—but their voices were not paid much heed at this time.

Knowing that King George approved, Lord North brought forward several proposals to the House of Commons. He suggested that it was necessary to:

☆ blockade the port of Boston till the tea was paid for,
☆ amend the Massachusetts Charter of 1691,
☆ ensure that royal justice would prevail by shipping prisoners to England for trial,
☆ move the capital of the province from Boston to Salem.

William Dowdeswell rose to speak against the measures:

This bill is unjust, unwise and dangerous. I therefore cannot permit it to pass as it has been requested with unanimity. All commerce may safely be carried on at Boston, but that in tea. We have heard no complaint from merchants. To do a thing merely because we have authority is absurd. It's only making a trial which shall get the better. I hope a bill will be moved [proposed] to take off the tea duty. Why is Boston singled out? At Philadelphia and New York commerce has been equally obstructed. The East India Company suffer by the return of the tea though not so much as if it was destroyed.[3]

Dowdeswell had warned against the tea duty in the first place, but now he warned against the Boston Port Act, which he said would punish the innocent along with the guilty. Edmund Burke made a similar speech, harping on the need to separate the guilty from the innocent: "I must give my total dissent to this bill. It's the most dangerous unjust one that ever was, and must I think be inefficacious. . . . I wish I may prove a false prophet when I say the example we are now going to make will be a dangerous one."[4]

Dowdeswell and Burke may both have been prophets, but the House of Commons was in a militant mood. Ever since 1765, when Americans had resisted the Stamp Act, England had seemed powerless to police her own colonies. Now, for the first time, it seemed possible to do so.

QUEBEC ACT

At about the same time that it considered Boston's punishment, the House of Commons took up the controversial subject of government in Quebec, which had been French Canada until the victories of 1759 and the Peace of Paris in 1763.

The French-Canadians had shown no inclination to give up their language, culture, or religion, so Lord North and the ministry proposed that they be allowed to retain them and that Quebec's land titles be expanded, so that it might serve as a check on the growing hinterland of the 13 American colonies. Most people who read the bill, or debated it, agreed that it was a progressive thing to do: Britain would show the superiority of her colonial system by allowing her new subjects to keep their culture. But they did not reckon on how Americans would feel.

MILITARY GOVERNMENT

Almost as soon as he heard of the Tea Party, King George decided on a strict measure to bring the American colonists to submission. Early in January, he had a long conversation with Lieutenant General Thomas Gage, who was the longtime commander of British troops in New York City. Gage had come to England for consultations, and the king provided him with an earful, saying that the colonists must be brought under British rule. Though he was married to an American woman, General

Gage was in complete agreement with his king. Days after the conversation, King George wrote to Lord North: "His language was very consonant to his character of an honest determined man. He says they will be lions, whilst we are lambs; but if we take the resolute part, they will undoubtedly prove very meek. He thinks the four regiments intended to relieve as many regiments in America, are sufficient to prevent any disturbance."[5]

King George went on to say that he regretted ever having rescinded the Stamp Act because ever since that time (1766) the Americans had proven much more obdurate. General Gage sailed for Boston in April 1774.

MORE TEA PARTIES

The American colonists had not been idle. Ever since news of the Tea Party had spread, the colonists had been more outspoken than before, voting resolutions in their town meetings and provincial legislatures at an almost frightening pace. The Committees of Correspondence made this easier, since legislators were able to profit by the example of their fellows in other colonies.

Annapolis, Maryland, had not been in the forefront of the move toward independence, but soon after the Tea Party its citizens took on a more militant aspect. In April 1774, they learned that a prominent merchant of the town, Anthony Stewart, had purchased a large amount of tea and was shipping it from London in the *Peggy Stewart*, named for his daughter. The people of Annapolis were immediately on their guard.

The people of Princeton, New Jersey, where the College of New Jersey was located, had already carried out a small "tea burning," consigning to the flames a small amount of tea that had been discovered. Something similar had been done in Boston, when a merchant of Dorchester was discovered concealing tea. There were even episodes in the hinterland, as in Montague, Massachusetts, where a local committee of safety ganged up on a harmless peddler, who was selling tea as he passed through. All this action seemed rather small, however, when compared to the news from London.

Boston had, meanwhile, carried out a second, much smaller Tea Party. In December 1773, there had actually been four ships aimed for Boston, but one of them, commanded by Captain Loring, had been cast away on the far side of

JONATHAN SINGLETON COPLEY

The greatest American painter of the eighteenth century split his life between Britain and America, so he is sometimes better remembered in the motherland than in the United States. Even so, anyone who looks at his vast body of portraiture will confess that here was a master of his art.

Copley was born in Boston in 1739, to a pair of Irish immigrants. His father died soon after he was born, and Copley was raised by his mother and his stepfather, Peter Pelham, a master engraver. There is no doubt that the stepfather's influence colored Copley's life, but also none that Copley was a native genius with brush, oil, and ink.

He began painting friends and neighbors in Boston, and his marriage in 1767 to a daughter of the merchant Richard Clarke won him more commissions. Copley was definitely a painter of the upper class: Very few poor or even middle-class folk were painted by him. In the five years before the Tea Party, he painted many of Boston's leading Loyalists—including some very beautiful women and girls—but he also painted John Hancock (1766), James Warren (1773), and even the arch incendiary, Samuel Adams. Given that the last of these subjects was the most famous, let us look at the results.

In the 1772 portrait, a year before the Tea Party, Samuel Adams stands before the viewer in a red coat; he looks more handsome, and less seedy, than he was in person. More impor-

Cape Cod. It took three months for the merchants involved to rescue the tea from that location, but their success seemed assured when it arrived at Boston in March 1774. The Sons of Liberty simply carried out another Tea Party, this time calling themselves Narragansett, and claiming that they were led by His Majesty Oknookortunkogog, as reported in the

tant, Adams carries in his left hand a scroll—which doubtless contains resolutions by the Boston town meeting—and he points to another scroll, lying on the table. This is known to be the 1691 Charter of the Province of Massachusetts Bay, which Bostonians of that time revered about as much as Americans today revere the Constitution of 1787. The overall impression is of a powerful, righteous man, who is reminding King George and Parliament that the Massachusetts colonists have rights.

In June 1774, Jonathan Singleton Copley and his wife and children went to London, along with his father-in-law (two years later, he executed a handsome portrait of the whole extended family). His career was exclusively British from that time on, and he painted patriotic scenes such as soldiers defending the Channel Islands against a French attack in 1779. Perhaps the most famous of all his paintings, on either side of the Atlantic, is entitled *Watson and the Shark*, displaying a man in a row boat doing battle with a shark. Watson was a real person, and—in the height of irony—he was one of the prominent merchants who had proposed that Richard Clarke and Sons be the consignees for tea in Boston.

Copley died in London in 1816. Many of his works hang in the Boston Museum of Fine Arts, located close to the public square named in his honor.

Boston Gazette. It was around this time that some rather fanciful poetry was written by Mercy Otis Warren, a prominent patriot who later wrote an entire history of the Revolutionary War. Ignoring all the talk about Mohawks and Narragansett, she chose to use the Tuscarora tribe of upstate New York for her inspiration for "The Squabble of the Sea Nymphs; or the Sacrifice of the Tuscaraoroes."

> The champions of the Tuscararan race. . . .
> Lent their strong arms in pity to the fair,
> To aid the bright Salacia's generous care,
> Pour's a profusion of delicious teas,
> Which, wafted by a soft savonian breeze,
> Supply's the wat'ry deities, in spite
> Of all the rage of jealous Amphyrite.
>
> The fair Salacia, victory, victory, sings,
> In spite of heroes, demi gods, or kings;
> She bids defiance to the servile train,
> The pimps and sychophants of George's reign.[6]

THE COERCIVE ACTS

General Thomas Gage landed at Boston on May 10, 1774. Bostonians who knew Gage and his American wife suspected he would be an easygoing governor, but the news he brought was almost catastrophic. The Port Bill had passed Parliament and received the assent of King George. The port of Boston was closed until the Bostonians paid for the tea they had destroyed (valued at anywhere between 11,000 and 18,000 pounds sterling).

Parliament had also passed the Administration of Justice Act, making it legal to transport British citizens to England for trial. The capital of Massachusetts had indeed been removed to Salem, and the Charter of 1691 had been amended so that towns could hold meetings only once a year.

General Thomas Gage (*above, on porch*) was initially welcomed in Massachusetts, but the new governor was under strict orders to remind the colonials that they were subjects of the British Empire.

SUPPORT FOR BOSTON

News of the Port Act reached other American coastal towns in May 1774, and many, if not most, American colonists showed distinct sympathy toward Boston. As far away as Williamsburg, Virginia, resolutions were taken in favor of Boston, and fasting days were proclaimed, so that all might share in Boston's pain. Merchants in Rhode Island announced their intention to ship food and winter clothing to Boston, so that its people would not suffer during the coming winter. King George had hoped, expected, that the other colonies would abandon Boston to her fate: This was not the case.

Ann Hulton, the sister of the British revenue collector, wrote from Boston to her London correspondent about how Boston was faring.

> I am sorry to say that there appears no disposition yet in the people towards complying with the Port Bill—They carry their molasses & other goods easily by land from Salem, & find little inconvience from its operation. The distress it will bring on the town will not be felt very severely before winter, when the roads will be impassible. There's little prospect of Boston Port being opened this year. The leaders of the faction are only more unwearied, & are pursuing every measure to draw the people onto resistance.[7]

PEGGY STEWART

Annapolis had been on guard for two months when the *Peggy Stewart* sailed in on October 14. The town's committee of safety had warned the populace, and Mr. Stewart came under increasing pressure to return his cargo to London. Stewart made a good case of self-defense, saying he had not known tea was aboard, but the pressure grew to where he decided to set the *Peggy Stewart* on fire, in front of the whole town, so everyone would know he had capitulated. One more scenario remained to be played out.

TEA BURNERS

In mid-December, some of the citizens of Cumberland County, New Jersey, learned that a merchant planned to ship tea overland, through the province, and bring it to market in Philadelphia. Given that many Americans still liked tea, it would be a sure success from a monetary point of view.

On December 27, the local committee of safety learned that the tea had been boarded in a warehouse in Greenwich; within hours, a mob had gathered, and the tea was brought forth from its hiding place and burned on the street. This "tea burners" event was commemorated by a statue, erected in 1909, and the residents of the town still celebrate the event each year.

In the autumn of 1774, the tea and tax policy of King George and Lord North was revealed as a complete and utter failure. Even the Stamp Act had not produced such unanimity among Americans; and even the Townshend Acts and the Boston Massacre had not produced what Americans now called the Continental Congress of 1774.

Nonconsumption, Nonimportation, Non-exportation

T he idea of a congress for the several colonies—as they were called—had been in the making for a few years, but it was the urgency of the Tea Party and the over-the-top response of the British government that brought it into being.

RODNEY

Caesar Rodney of Maryland generally does not receive as much attention as other revolutionaries of his time, but in May 1774 he was the first to propose a truly continental congress, one that would embrace all the British colonies on the American continent (of course that left out Newfoundland, British Flor-ida, and French-speaking Quebec). Rodney put forth the idea that an attack—whether economic or military—on one colony was an attack on all the others, and, in his wake, other colonial leaders called for a Continental Congress. No special record

On September 5, 1774, 58 delegates from the British colonies in America met in Philadelphia for the first ever Continental Congress. Many prominent business and political leaders attended this meeting, including Benjamin Franklin, John Adams, and George Washington.

was made of the elections, and it is safe to assume that many of the delegates that went to Philadelphia were simply appointed by the colonial legislatures. When they met in Philadelphia, on Monday, September 5, 1774, there were 58 delegates.

COMPOSITION

There were two delegates from New Hampshire, two from Rhode Island, three from Connecticut, and four from Massachusetts, which sent Thomas Cushing (often the moderator of the Boston Town Meeting), Samuel Adams, John Adams, and Robert Treat Paine. The colony of New York sent four delegates, but the county of Suffolk, also in New York, sent another. Maryland sent three, Delaware, which was still called the counties on the Delaware River, sent three, New Jersey sent five, Virginia sent seven (including George Washington), six came from Pennsylvania, and five from South Carolina. Georgia, as had been its wont ever since the Stamp Act, did not condescend to send delegates.

The first order of business was to elect a president of the proceedings: Peyton Randolph of Virginia was elected unanimously. The delegates went to work reading all sorts of resolves and resolutions, written by towns, committees, and sometimes whole colonies. Almost everyone, it seemed, had an idea of how the Continental Congress should go about its business.

SUFFOLK RESOLVES

In the meantime, Suffolk County, Massachusetts, had penned a series of resolves that built both upon the Philadelphia Town Meeting of the previous year and on the many articles and pamphlets written against the tax on tea. Paul Revere was again asked to be the express messenger of the Boston Committee of Correspondence. He rode from Boston to Philadelphia in about six days to present the Suffolk Resolves.

The Suffolk Resolves echoed much that had been said and written over the previous 12 months. They did not specifically

SAMUEL JOHNSON'S TAKE ON THE COLONIES

One of the most poignant answers to the Suffolk Resolves, and to the deliberations of the First Continental Congress, came from the pen of Samuel Johnson, England's most famous wit and political philosopher.

> While we are melting in silent sorrow, and in the transports of delicious pity, dropping both the sword and balance from our hands, another friend of the Americans thinks it better to awaken another passion, and tries to alarm our interest, or excite our veneration, by accounts of their greatness and their opulence, of the fertility of their land, and the splendor of their towns.*

Johnson then lampooned American virtues:

> We are then told that the Americans, however wealthy, cannot be taxed; that they are the descendants of men who left all for liberty, and that they have constantly preserved the principles and stubbornness of their progenitors; that they are too obstinate for persuasion, and too powerful for constraint; that they will laugh at argument, and defeat violence; that the continent of North America contains three millions, not of men merely, but of Whigs, of Whigs fierce for liberty, and disdainful of dominion; that they multiply with the fecundity of their own rattle-snakes, so that every quarter of a century doubles their numbers.**

Johnson was clearly in a venomous mood when he penned these lines, but his passion does not detract from the logic of his argument.

(continues)

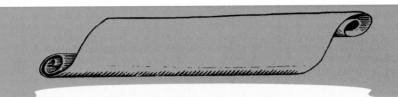

(continued)

All men (and women) he wrote, had to make the painful choice between the freedoms afforded by nature and the constraints imposed by government: The Americans were no different.

> Before they quit the comforts of a warm home [in Boston] for the founding something which they think better, he cannot be thought their enemy who advises them to consider well whether they shall find it. By turning fishermen or hunters, woodmen or shepherd, they may become wild, but it is not so easy to conceive them free; for who can be more a slave than he that is driven by force from the comforts of life, is compelled to leave his house to a casual comer, and whatever he does, or wherever he wanders, finds every moment some new testimony of his own subjection. If the choice of evil is freedom, the felon in the gallies has his option of labor or stripes. The Bostonian may quit his house to starve in the fields; his dog may refuse to set, and smart under the lash, and they may then congratulate each other upon the smiles of liberty, *profuse with bliss, and pregnant with delight* [emphasis in the original].***

Johnson had much more to say; his pamphlet ran to 80 pages. But his essential message to the Americans was that the so-called tyranny of King George and the Parliament was far preferable to the whims of nature, to which rebellion would bring them.

---

* Johnson, Samuel. *Taxation No Tyranny*. London: 1775, pp. 5–6.
** Ibid., pp. 6–7.
*** Ibid., pp. 11–12.

call for independence from Britain, but they spoke of no obedi-ence being due to a wicked judiciary, a rigged Parliament, and a monarch out of touch with the American people. They fulmi-nated against the Quebec Act, and claimed it was part of an over-all plot to bring Boston and Massachusetts into full submission. So much was said about the fortifications being built around Boston that the Continental Congress sent a letter to General Gage, asking if these were defensive or offensive in nature.

IMPORTATION AND CONSUMPTION

The delegates who came to Philadelphia were, on the whole, sober men of business and trade. Rather few of them expected to make a radical severance with the British motherland, but almost none of them believed the current condition could continue. There had to be some type of adjustment between Britain and the colonies. The most sensible plan was put for-ward by Joseph Galloway of Pennsylvania, who called for an Act of Union between England and the colonies, along the lines of what had unified England and Scotland in 1707. This plan drew the most support, and the First Continental Congress sent a number of rather supplicatory letters to King George. The most important ones were all sent at the end of October. First, the Continental Congress addressed King George:

> That from and after the first day of December next, we will not import, into British America, from Great Britain or Ire-land, any goods, wares of merchandise whatsoever. . . .
>
> We will neither import nor purchase any slave imported after the first day of December. . . .
>
> We, as above, solemnly agree and associate, that, from this day, we will not purchase or use any tea, imported on account of the East India company.[1]

This was much stronger than the boycotts of the late 1760s. It was a nonconsumption, nonimportation, non-exportation movement. Just to make certain everyone understood the severity of the situation, the Continental Congress declared that the committees of correspondence would be empowered to search the custom houses, and that the 12 colonies that signed this agreement (all except Georgia) would have no "trade, commerce, dealings, or intercourse whatsoever"[2] with any colony that did not adhere to the agreement, and that its citizens would be held "unworthy of the rights of freemen, and as inimical to the liberties of their country."[3]

The Association was signed by 52 members of the Continental Congress.

TO THE PEOPLE

The Continental Congress went on to send a letter addressed to the people of Great Britain. The authors extolled the blessings of liberty that the British people had obtained over the centuries since the Magna Carta had been signed in 1215. They went on to say that Englishmen who had never allowed their liberties to be trampled should not be surprised that Americans—who descended from the same common stock—should refuse to pay the unjust taxes of a ministry that seemed determined to put chains upon the colonies. This read rather well, but the authors were disingenuous when it came to the matter of the Tea Party. They declared:

> While the town was suspended by deliberations on this important subject, the tea was destroyed. Even supposing a trespass was thereby committed, and the proprietors of the tea entitled to damages—the courts of law were open and the judges appointed by the crown presided in them—the East India Company however did not think proper to commence any suits, nor did they even demand satisfaction.[4]

It must have been obvious to anyone reading this open letter that the East India Company did not sue because its directors knew they could not obtain justice in an American court.

TO THE AMERICAN PEOPLE

The Continental Congress then addressed a memorial to the inhabitants of the colonies. After reviewing the long history of taxes and customs duties, the Continental Congress declared that Britain must make amends for her past behavior. The address ended: "Above all things we earnestly intreat you, with devotion of spirit, penitence of heart, and amendment of life, to humble yourselves, and implore the favor of almighty God: and we fervently beseech his divine goodness, to take you into his gracious protection."[5]

TO THE CANADIAN PEOPLE

There was one more letter to write: this one to the French-Canadians.

Just 15 years earlier, the American colonists had regarded the Catholic French Canadians as a dangerous people, whose interests were diametrically opposed to their own. Now, however, believing that the British ministry was determined to make slaves of the English-speaking colonies, the Continental Congress sent an open letter to the people of Quebec, listing the rights that were being deprived by Lord North and his fellow ministers. These were:

> freedom of the press,
> the right of trial by jury,
> the right of freeholders to their lands,
> the right to representation in the supreme legislature.

Knowing that they could be accused of inciting treason among their northern neighbors, the leaders of the Continental Congress used these words: "We do not ask you, by this address, to commence acts of hostility against the government of our common sovereign. We only invite you to consult your own glory and welfare, and not to suffer yourselves to be inveigled or intimidated by infamous ministers so far, as to become the instruments of their cruelty or despotism."[6]

Then came the surprise:

"We submit it to your consideration, whether it may not be expedient for you to meet together in your several towns and districts, and elect deputies, to represent your province in the continental congress to be held at Philadelphia on the tenth day of May, 1775."[7]

Truly, the men meeting in Philadelphia wished this to be a continental congress.

WINTER

The delegates to the Continental Congress went home at the end of October, having resolved to meet again in the spring. During the winter, Boston continued to spin out of control.

General Gage's letters to Lord Dartmouth became increasingly anxious. At first, he believed that four regiments would be enough to pacify Massachusetts; then he upped it to 10,000 men; and by the later winter he increased the number to 20,000. Even the great British Empire would have a difficult time providing that many troops, especially if they were required to subdue one province, all on its own.

RESOLUTION

King George became increasingly set in his mind, determined that the colonists must be forced to submit. His orders to General Gage—sent in the late winter of 1775—instructed the general to confiscate the gunpowder and ammunition of the rebels in and around Boston. Gage knew it to be a nearly impossible task, but, like a good soldier, he set his plans in motion. On the evening of April 18, 1775, about 1,500 British soldiers were lined up near their rowboats on the northwest side of Boston, ready to cross the Charles River and march into the country towns.

PAUL REVERE'S RIDE

Paul Revere had been a busy man for some time, running messages for the Committees of Correspondence, the Boston Town Meeting, and others. On the evening of April 18, he planned one

When British soldiers arrived to seize weapons and gunpowder from rebelling colonists in the countryside, Paul Revere was alerted to their presence. Revere, who sighted two signal lamps hung in the Old North Church, rode off to spread the message that the British were coming by sea.

last ride, to let the people of the countryside know that the British were coming. To the best of our knowledge, he did not shout those exact words, but rather, "The regulars are coming out!"[8]

Revere was on the Charlestown side of the river when someone placed two lamps in the belfry of the Old North Church (very near his house) to let him know that the British were coming by sea (the Charles River) rather than by land (The Neck). Once he saw those signal lights, Revere galloped off into the darkness to awaken the farmers of Middlesex County.

Fourteen years had passed since the coronation of King George III, a time when British-American relations were at their best.

Ten years had passed since Parliament laid the Stamp Act on the colonies, and nine years since the Stamp Act had been rescinded.

Eight years had passed since the creation of the Townshend Revenue Acts, and five years since the Boston Massacre.

All these events had led Americans into conflict with their British cousins. All of them had led to suspicion between the colonies and the motherland. The Tea Party, on December 16, 1773, was the straw that broke the camel's back. When British regulars and American militiamen clashed on Lexington Green, at seven in the morning on April 19, 1775, they were enacting the last act of a play that had begun with the succession of George III to the throne. The colonists were English-Americans no more: They were well on their way to becoming Americans.

Evolution of
the Tea Party

At first, people did not call it the "Tea Party." Those words came many years after the event. When the American Revolution began, on April 19, 1775, many observers, especially Europeans, believed that Britain would subdue the colonies quite rapidly. The reputation of the British redcoat was formidable.

There were rough times for the colonies (which became states with the Declaration of Independence in 1776), but by 1778, quite a few foreign observers believed that the Americans had a chance: They might win their political independence. It was around this time that a famous print was made, in France; it soon found its way to other European nations and to the American states.

TEA-TAX TEMPEST

The print shows Britain as a woman, perhaps the goddess Minerva, in the foreground, with another woman, perhaps one

The escalating tensions between the colonists and the British govern-ment culminated in the American Revolutionary War. Men throughout the colonies organized themselves into militias and fought against the British army in battles located in Quebec, Yorktown (*above*), and other places throughout the colonies.

of the Muses, consoling her for the recent difficulties. To their left crouches a Native American, complete with headdress and quiver of arrows. He faces toward the center of the print, away from the viewer. His attention, like that of the viewer, is directed by a winged figure that represents Father Time, who has his left hand on a globe, and his right hand and finger point attention to a scene that he illuminates with what can only be called a magic lamp.

That scene shows patriotic Americans on the right, Loyalist Americans on the left, and a huge explosion separating the two. The explosion is set off by an enormous pot of tea, and whether they are sparks or blasts of liquid that come forth is difficult to say. A rooster sits near the teapot. Most likely this represents France, or the Gallic Cock, as it was often portrayed. At the time this print was made, France was about to enter the American Revolution as an ally of the newly made American states.

The entire scene has an operatic feel to it: One can sense the cords and pulleys that will bring down the curtain at some moment. One feels that the artist presents a picture of how dramatic the Tea Party (still not employing that name) was for Americans, Britons, and Europeans who looked on the scene with a certain wonder. How could so innocent a thing as tea, and so small a number as three pence, make such a "tempest in a tea pot" (an expression that entered the English language around that time)?

Historians have wrestled with that question ever since.

DESTRUCTION OF THE TEA

For at least a generation after 1773, Bostonians and other Americans called the event the Destruction of the Tea. This was the name used in letters, diaries, and by those who sought to commemorate the event. But there were so many other notable events from the 1770s and 1780s—including the battles of Trenton, Saratoga, and Yorktown—that over time people forgot about the Destruction of the Tea. The Boston Massacre continued to be perpetuated in anniversary remembrances, but very few people came together to celebrate the Tea Party; indeed, there was a strong reluctance to do so. As late as about 1820, when asked, John Adams said that the names of the participants were not known and never would be revealed to the public.

It was around this time that the name Destruction of the Tea began to yield to the Tea Party.

The Tea-Tax Tempest, or
Ungewitter entstanden durch die
Orage causé par l'Impôt

the Anglo-American Revolution.
Stichtage mit den Thee in Amerika.
sur le Thé en Amérique.

In *The Tea-Tax Tempest*, Old Father Time is perched behind a globe, show-ing representatives of the world how patriotic colonists gained their free-dom from the British Crown by uniting behind the issue of tea.

NOSTALGIA

Many of the leading Bostonian radicals died in the early part of the nineteenth century. Samuel Adams died in 1803; Paul Revere in 1818; and John Adams—the longest lived of the group—died on July 4, 1826, the fiftieth anniversary of the Declaration of Independence. During the 1820s and 1830s, many Americans felt nostalgia for the Revolutionary time and generation, and they sought to perpetuate its memory. The

Bunker Hill Monument, in Charlestown, Massachusetts, was dedicated in 1843, and other memories of the American Revolution and its men were created around the country (women's contributions to the war effort went underreported).

In Boston and New York, towns that treasured their American Revolution connection, there was also a movement among the working class and underprivileged to assert that the Revolution belonged to them, as well as to the upper class. Paintings by artists like Jonathan Trumball, for example, represented the Revolution as having been largely been fought by merchants, lawyers, and what Thomas Jefferson called the natural aristocracy of the United States. Not so! the working-class leaders asserted.

In 1833, for the sixtieth anniversary of the Tea Party (it was around this time that it gained that name), Boston made an effort to bring together people from that time. Only one or two could be positively identified; one was George Robert Twelve Hewes, who was now living in upstate New York. Hewes came to Boston to participate in the celebrations and at least two paintings were executed, one of which seems much more realistic. Hewes was celebrated by Bostonians as a man of the people, one of the unsung heroes that had come out to destroy the tea and thereby launch the 13 colonies in the direction of the American Revolution.

Not one but two books were written on Hewes, one published in 1834 and the second a year later. Both were written in a journalistic style, as the authors wished their readers to hear about this paragon of virtue from the time of their grandfathers. *Traits of the Tea-Party, Being a Memoir of George R.T. Hewes*, concludes with a paragraph about the times of 1773 and how the present generation should preserve them:

> Boston is full of spots "steeped with the hues of sacrifice."
> Let them be marked out, and consecrated to everlasting
> homage, ere it is too late. The site of the Massacre is one.

That of the Tea-Party is another. If no graven column shall rise upon that ground, to utter its silent eulogy of the brave men who hazarded their all for us, let not the imputation rest upon us that we know not, or dare not avow, the place. Griffin's Wharf! Let the good old name, at least, be restored, and preserved forever![1]

THE MAJOR PARTICIPANTS

Thomas Hutchinson left his beloved Massachusetts in June 1774, never to return. He met with King George, was well received by the British government, and was the acknowledged leader of the American Loyalists in London until his death in 1780.

James Otis, who argued against the writs of assistance and wrote the pamphlet *The Rights of the British Colonies Asserted and Proved*, went insane in the last decade of his life. He died in 1783 after being struck by lightning.

Samuel Adams was the number-one patriot in the years leading up to the American Revolution, but he ceded that position to his second cousin John Adams during the war itself. Samuel Adams was elected governor of Massachusetts five times. He died in Boston in 1803.

Paul Revere encountered difficulty in the Revolutionary War. As Colonel Revere, and a leader of a naval expedition to Maine, in 1779, he came in for criticism and even a court-martial, at which he was exonerated. Revere lived in Boston's North End until his death in 1818; toward the end, he was seen as the last of the patriots of 1773, thanks to his wearing a tricorn hat and Revolutionary-style clothing to the end.

John Adams became a leading member of the Second Continental Congress, an ambassador to Holland and then France,

INTERPRETATIONS

In the early part of the twentieth century, the Tea Party became a fixture in schoolbooks, but it is questionable whether Americans understood much about the event. It seemed too light-hearted to belong to the grimmer times associated with lost battles and campaigns of the Revolution. The two hundredth

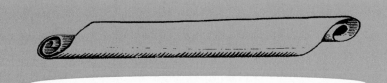

vice president of the United States (1789–1797), and finally president (1797–1801). He retired to Quincy, Massachusetts, where he lived to the ripe age of 91.

King George lived until 1820, but he was mentally unstable for the last 20 years of his life. His good friend, Frederick Lord North, died in 1784. Edmund Burke, who spoke on behalf of the colonies—time and again—became the most noted British political philosopher of his time. His *Reflections on the Revolution in France* (1791) has been hailed as one of the most important works of the eighteenth century.

Jonathan Singleton Copley had, perhaps, the most fortunate life of any of the actors in the Tea Party. Having achieved great fame as an American painter, he moved to London in 1775 and became equally famous—perhaps more so—in Britain.

George Robert Twelve Hewes served on an American privateer ship during the American Revolution. He later moved to upstate New York, where journalists found him in 1833, in time for the celebration of the sixtieth anniversary of the Tea Party.

Little is known of Ann Hulton's life after she left Boston in 1775. Her brother, Henry Hulton, later served as a British commissioner in Nova Scotia.

anniversary of the Tea Party, in 1973, naturally stirred some attention, but it took the writings of historian Alfred F. Young to really bring the event back to life.

One of the foremost historians of the Revolutionary period, Young rediscovered the writings of the two men who interviewed George Robert Twelve Hewes. Through their work, and by piecing together other bits of evidence, Young was able to posit a new thesis: The common, underpaid workers of Boston not only played a major part in the Tea Party, but also in the resistance to the Stamp Act and Townshend Acts. Young's *The Shoemaker and the Tea Party*, published in 1999, was a seminal work, and many younger scholars began working in similar directions, to find out what was unknown about the working class of America's colonial and Revolutionary towns.

Young's work was followed, in 2004, by a major scholarly effort by T.H. Breen (it is worth noting that both Young and Breen taught at midwestern colleges, not eastern ones). In *The Marketplace of Revolution*, Breen showed how Americans of the 1760s and early 1770s began to reject British goods—as part of nonimportation—and demonstrated how that was the first step toward rejecting British government. Breen made many interesting discoveries, not the least of which was the way tea was perceived by Americans after the Tea Party. What had once been a pleasurable beverage and a sign of the connection to the motherland became a symbol of tyranny, even of absolute government. By September 1774, when the delegates to the Continental Congress assembled, a new American mentality—one forged at least in part by consumer politics—had developed.

THE TWO HUNDRED FIFTIETH ANNIVERSARY

The two hundred fiftieth anniversary of the Tea Party will be celebrated in 2023, a time when the United States will have weathered storms even greater than those known to the men and women of 1773. America has grown from 13 colonies to 50 states, but much of the growth was due to the sacrifices of men like Samuel Adams, John Adams, James Otis, and George Robert Twelve Hewes. The activities of women of the time are less known, but the boycotts of 1765, the nonimportation of 1768, and then the nonconsumption movement of 1774 all would have faltered if American women had continued to purchase British goods. Then, too, there are the writings of women like Mercy Otis Warren.

It is difficult to say how the Tea Party will be viewed by future generations. For almost 150 years it has been seen as a frolic, an entertainment, but the people of 1773 knew better. To destroy the East India Company tea was akin to slapping the British government in the face. Boston took that risk, and, to the surprise of many, other towns and colonies followed suit. The rest belongs to memory.

CHRONOLOGY

1757 Robert Clive wins the Battle of Plassey, ensuring Britain will dominate in India.

1759 James Wolfe wins the Battle of Quebec, ensuring Britain will dominate in Canada.

1760 George, the Prince of Wales, becomes King George III on the death of his grandfather.

1761 James Otis of Boston argues against the writs of assistance.

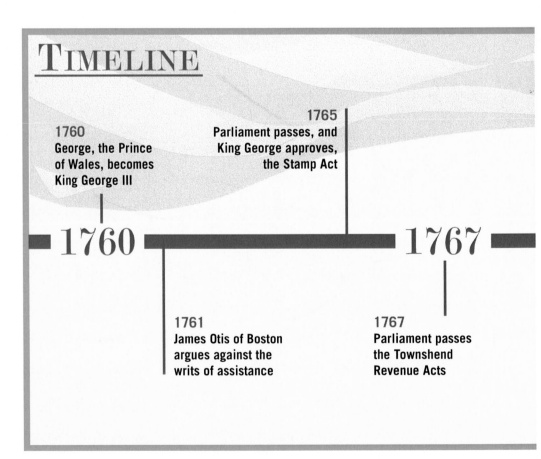

TIMELINE

1760
George, the Prince of Wales, becomes King George III

1765
Parliament passes, and King George approves, the Stamp Act

1760

1767

1761
James Otis of Boston argues against the writs of assistance

1767
Parliament passes the Townshend Revenue Acts

1763   The Peace of Paris confirms the British victories in the Seven Years' War.

1764   Parliament amends the Sugar Act to make collection easier.

1765   Parliament passes, and King George approves, the Stamp Act.

There are major protests throughout the American colonies.

1766   The Stamp Act is repealed.

The Declaratory Act is passed and approved.

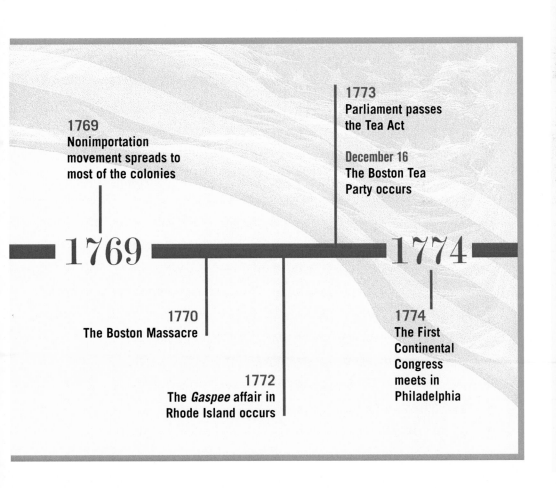

1769
Nonimportation movement spreads to most of the colonies

1773
Parliament passes the Tea Act

December 16
The Boston Tea Party occurs

1769

1774

1770
The Boston Massacre

1772
The *Gaspee* affair in Rhode Island occurs

1774
The First Continental Congress meets in Philadelphia

1767   Parliament passes the Townshend Revenue Acts.

1768   Ann Hulton arrives in Boston with her brother and his family.

John Hancock's sloop *Liberty* is seized in Boston Harbor.

Two regiments arrive in Boston on October 1.

1769   Nonimportation movement spreads to most of the colonies.

1770   Parliament removes four out of five of the Townshend Acts.

The Boston Massacre occurs.

There is a trial of soldiers involved in the Boston Massacre.

1772   The *Gaspee* affair in Rhode Island occurs.

Lord Dartmouth becomes secretary of state for the colonies.

1773   Thomas Hutchinson's letters are revealed to the public.

Parliament passes the Tea Act, to assist the East India Company.

News of the Tea Act reaches the colonies; Philadelphia and New York resist; Boston mobilizes.

December 16 The Boston Tea Party occurs.

1774   The *Peggy Stewart* is burned at Annapolis.

Coercive Acts are passed by Parliament.

General Thomas Gage arrives in Boston.

1774   The First Continental Congress meets in Philadelphia.

Cumberland County Tea Burners destroy tea in New Jersey.

1775   The Revolutionary War begins with the battles of Lexington and Concord.

NOTES

CHAPTER 1

1. *Letters of a Loyalist Lady, Being the Letters of Ann Hulton, Sister of Henry Hulton, Commissioner of Customs at Boston, 1767–1776.* Cambridge, Mass.: Harvard University Press, 1927, p. 11.
2. Ibid.
3. Ibid.
4. Ibid.
5. Ibid., p. 15.
6. Ibid., p. 17.

CHAPTER 2

1. *Boston Gazette and Country News Letter*, October 16, 1767.
2. Ibid., November 23, 1767.

CHAPTER 3

1. Stewart, I.N. Phelps, and Daniel C. Haskell, editors. *American Historical Prints.* New York: New York Public Library, 1932, p. 40.
2. Breen, T.H. *The Marketplace Revolution: How Consumer Politics Shaped American Independence.* New York: Oxford University Press, 2004, p. 195.
3. *A Retrospect of the Boston Tea Party, with a memoir of George R.T. Hewes*, by a citizen of New York. New York: S.S. Bliss Printer, 1834, p. 28.
4. Simmons, R.C., and P.D.G. Thomas, editors. *Proceedings and Debates of the British Parliaments Respecting North America*, volume 3. Millwood,

N.Y.: Kraus International, 1984, p. 258.
5. *Legal Papers of John Adams*, edited by Kinvin Wroth and Hiller B. Zobel, volume 3. Cambridge, Mass.: Harvard University Press, 1965, p. 266.
6. Ibid.

CHAPTER 4

1. *Copy of Letters Sent to Great Britain by his Excellency Thomas Hutchinson.* Boston: Edes and Gill, 1773, p. 16.
2. Ibid.
3. Simmons and Thomas, *Proceedings and Debates*, p. 488.

CHAPTER 5

1. Drake, Francis S. *Tea Leaves, Being a Collection of Letters and Documents Relating to the Shipment of Tea.* Boston, 1884, reprinted in 1970. Detroit: Singing Tree Press, pp. 230–231.
2. *Pennsylvania Packet*, December 8, 1773.
3. *Letters of a Loyalist Lady*, p. 64.
4. Davies, K.G., editor. *Documents of the American Revolution, 1770–1783*, volume 6. Dublin, Ireland: Irish University Press, 1974, p. 255.
5. Ibid., p. 265.
6. *Traits of the Tea Party; Being a Memoir of George R.T. Hewes*, by a Bostonian. New York: Harper & Brothers, 1835, pp. 259–160.
7. Ibid., p. 260.

CHAPTER 6

1. *Traits of the Tea Party*, pp. 259–260.
2. Ibid., p. 260.
3. Lowance, Mason I., and Georgia B. Bumgardner, editors. *Massachusetts Broadsides of the American Revolution.* Amherst: University of Massachusetts Press, 1976, p. 37.
4. Ibid.
5. Ibid.
6. Stoll, Ira. *Samuel Adams: A Life.* New York: The Free Press, 2008, p. 114.
7. Lowance and Bumgardner, editors. *Massachusetts Broadsides*, p. 38.
8. Ibid.
9. Drake, *Tea Leaves*, p. LVII.
10. Stoll, Ira. *Samuel Adams*, p. 115.

CHAPTER 7

1. Griswold, Welsey. *The Night the Revolution Began: The Boston Tea Party.* Brattleboro, Vt.: Stephen Greene Press, p.92.
2. *A Retrospect of the Boston Tea Party, with a Memoir of George R.T. Hewes,* by a citizen of New York. New York: S.S. Bliss Printer, 1834, pp. 40–41.
3. Griswold, *The Night the Revolution Began*, p. 105.
4. Ibid., p. 106.
5. Labraree, Benjamin Woods. *The Boston Tea Party.* New York: Oxford University Press, 1964, p. 145.

6. *Pennsylvania Gazette and Packet,* December 27, 1773.
7. *Boston Gazette and Country Journal,* December 27, 1773.

CHAPTER 8

1. *Letters of a Loyalist Lady*, p. 69.
2. Ibid., pp. 69–70.
3. Simmons and Thomas, *Proceedings and Debates*, p. 135.
4. Ibid., p. 136.
5. Mumby, Frank Arthur. *George III and the American Revolution: The Beginnings.* London: Constable & Company, 1924, p. 323.
6. *The Plays and Poems of Mercy Otis Warren.* Delmar, N.Y.: Scholars' Facsimiles & Reprints, 1980, pp. 204–205.
7. *Letters of a Loyalist Lady*, p. 73.

CHAPTER 9

1. *Journals of the Continental Congress, 1774–1789,* edited by Worthington Chauncey Ford. Washington DC Government Printing Office, 1904, pp. 78–79.
2. Ibid., p. 79.
3. Ibid.
4. Ibid., p. 86.
5. Ibid., p. 101.
6. Ibid., p. 112.
7. Ibid.
8. Fischer, David Hackett. *Paul Revere's Ride.* New York: Oxford University Press, 1994, p. 109.

CHAPTER 10

1. *Traits of the Tea Party*, pp. 252–253.

BIBLIOGRAPHY

A Retrospect of the Boston Tea Party, with a Memoir of George R.T. Hewes, by a citizen of New York. New York: S.S. Bliss Printer, 1834.

Bailyn, Bernard. *The Ordeal of Thomas Hutchinson.* Cambridge, Mass.: Harvard University Press, 1974.

Bourne, Russell. *Cradle of Violence: How Boston's Waterfront Mobs Ignited the American Revolution.* New York: John Wiley & Sons, 2006.

Breen, T.H. *The Marketplace Revolution: How Consumer Politics Shaped American Independence.* New York: Oxford University Press, 2004.

Davies, K.G., editor. *Documents of the American Revolution, 1770–1783,* volume 6. Dublin, Ireland: Irish University Press, 1974.

Drake, Francis S. *Tea Leaves, Being a Collection of Letters and Documents Relating to the Shipment of Tea.* Boston, 1884, reprinted. Detroit: Singing Tree Press, 1970.

Hulton, Ann. *Letters of a Loyalist Lady, Being the Letters of Ann Hulton, Sister of Henry Hulton, Commissioner of Customs at Boston, 1767–1776.* Cambridge, Mass.: Harvard University Press, 1927.

Journals of the Continental Congress, 1774–1789, edited by Worthington Chauncey Ford. Washington, D.C.: Government Printing Office, 1904.

Labaree, Benjamin Woods. *The Boston Tea Party.* New York: Oxford University Press, 1964.

Legal Papers of John Adams, edited by Kinvin Wroth and Hiller B. Zobel. volume 3. Cambridge, Mass.: Harvard University Press, 1965.

Lowance, Mason I., and Georgia B. Bumgardner, editors. *Massachusetts Broadsides of the American Revolution*. Amherst: University of Massachusetts Press, 1976.

Morison, S.E., editor. *Sources and Documents Illustrating the American Revolution, 1764–1788*. Oxford, England: The Clarendon Press, 1923.

Norris, Walter B. *Annapolis: Its Colonial and Naval Story*. New York: Thomas Y. Crowell Company, 1925.

The Plays and Poems of Mercy Otis Warren. Delmar, N.Y.: Scholars' Facsimiles & Reprints, 1980.

FURTHER READING

Fischer, David Hackett. *Paul Revere's Ride.* New York: Oxford University Press, 1994.

Griswold, Welsey. *The Night the Revolution Began: The Boston Tea Party.* Brattleboro, Vt.: Stephen Greene Press.

Patton, Robert H. *Patriot Pirates: The Privateer War for Freedom and Fortune in the American Revolution.* New York: Knopf, Doubleday, 2009.

Pearson, Michael. *Those Damned Rebels: The American Revolution as Seen through British Eyes.* New York: G.P. Putnam's Sons, 1972.

Stoll, Ira. *Samuel Adams: A Life.* New York: The Free Press, 2008.

Young, Alfred F. *The Shoemaker and the Tea Party.* Boston: Beacon Press, 1999.

WEB SITES
Boston Tea Party Ship and Museum

http://www.bostonteapartyship.com/

This is the most famous historical commemoration of the Tea Party.

Gaspee Virtual Archives

http://www.gaspee.org/

A collection of primary sources relating to the destruction of the *Gaspee* in 1772.

Loyalist Collection at the University of New Brunswick

http://www.lib.unb.ca/collections/loyalist/seeOne.php?id=647&string=

A short film about Henry Hulton, commissioner of customs at Boston, 1767–1776.

Old South Meeting House

http://www.oldsouthmeetinghouse.org/default.aspx

Web site describes current activity at the Old South Meeting House, and provides information for possible historical research.

The Peggy Stewart

http://www.mdoe.org/peggystewart.html

Web site describes the destruction of the *Peggy Stewart* in August 1774.

Tea Burners Reenactment, Cumberland County Historical Society

http://www.cchistsoc.org/teaburnerscelebration.html

Each year the burning of tea in Greenwich, New Jersey, is commemorated.

Photo Credits

INDEX

ABOUT THE AUTHOR

SAMUEL WILLARD CROMPTON lives about 100 miles west of Boston, in the Berkshire Hills, an area that demonstrated plenty of opposition to King George and the customs men. A town six miles from him is named for a Revolutionary-era merchant who was forced, by his neighbors, to submit to Massachusetts-style politics, and to swear off his allegiance to king and Parliament. Crompton teaches history at Holyoke Community College. He is the author of a number of books, and is a major contributor to the *American National Biography*.